TOYS OR PHYSICS?

EXPLAINING PHYSICS THROUGH TOYS

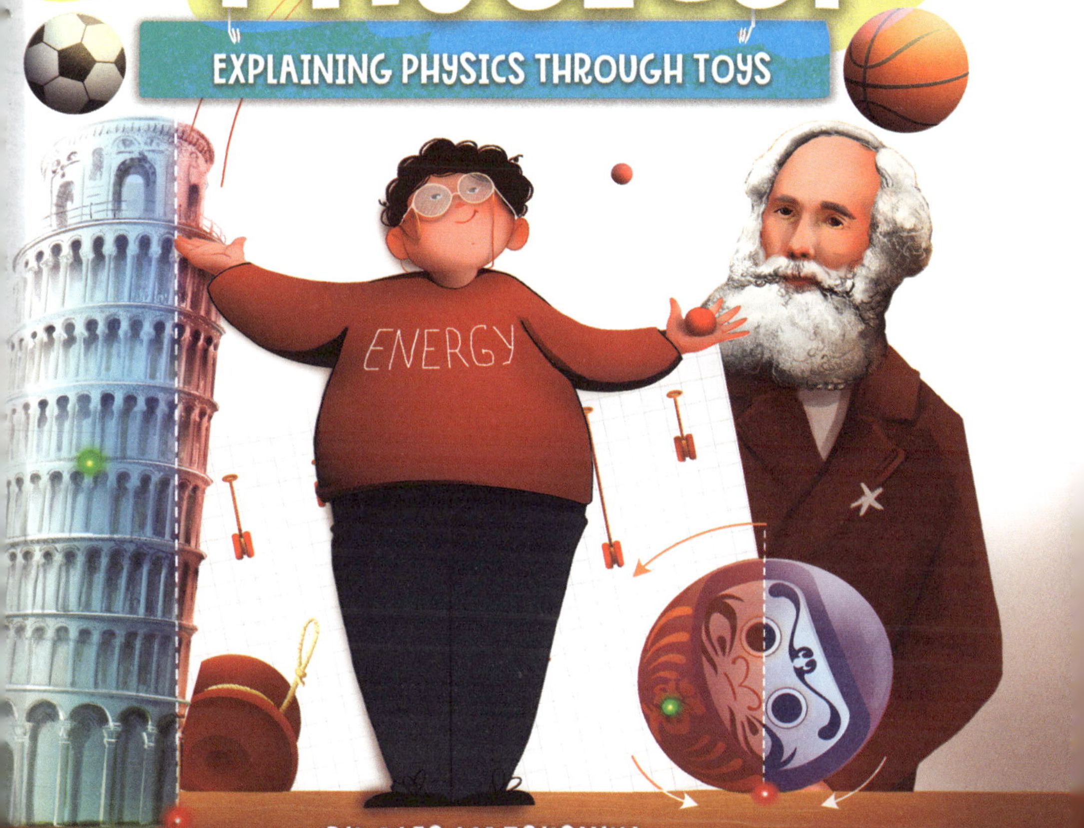

BY OLES MATSYSHYN
ILLUSTRATIONS BY KATERYNA MARTYNIUK

WS Education
NEW JERSEY • LONDON • SINGAPORE • BEIJING • SHANGHAI • HONG KONG • TAIPEI • CHENNAI • TOKYO

Published by
WS Education, an imprint of
World Scientific Publishing Co. Pte. Ltd.
5 Toh Tuck Link, Singapore 596224
USA office: 27 Warren Street, Suite 401-402, Hackensack, NJ 07601
UK office: 57 Shelton Street, Covent Garden, London WC2H 9HE

British Library Cataloguing-in-Publication Data
A catalogue record for this book is available from the British Library.

TOYS OR PHYSICS?
Explaining Physics Through Toys

ISBN 978-981-128-150-1 (hardcover)
ISBN 978-981-128-151-8 (paperback)
ISBN 978-981-128-152-5 (ebook for institutions)
ISBN 978-981-128-153-2 (ebook for individuals)

Desk Editor: Daniele Lee

Printed in Singapore

This book was created with the help of the Max Planck Institute for the Physics of Complex Systems in Dresden, Germany.

CONTENTS

FOREWORD

In a nutshell, this book is about physics. Its primary purpose is to amaze readers, familiarise them with the basics of physics and spark an interest in science. Within the book, you will find 17 chapters examining various aspects of physics through the use of different toys.

Some of the explanations you will come across in this book involve rules that we call the laws of physics. These laws were learnt over time as people observed that some things always happened the same way. The science of physics was founded on observation, and one of the most important ways that we learn new things is by conducting experiments.

Are you ready to begin? We are now going to learn about the first fundamental law of physics: the law of conservation of energy. We will do this by exploring our first toy, the super ball.

SUPER BALL

WHAT'S THAT TOY?

The super ball was invented in 1964 by chemist Norman Stingley. It is small, rubbery, elastic and can be thrown, just like any other ball.

However, unlike most other balls, the super ball bounces back to nearly the same height it was dropped from. In other words, it doesn't lose much of its "energy" (height) as it bounces. Most other balls – such as soccer balls or basketballs – would stop bouncing after hitting the floor a few times.

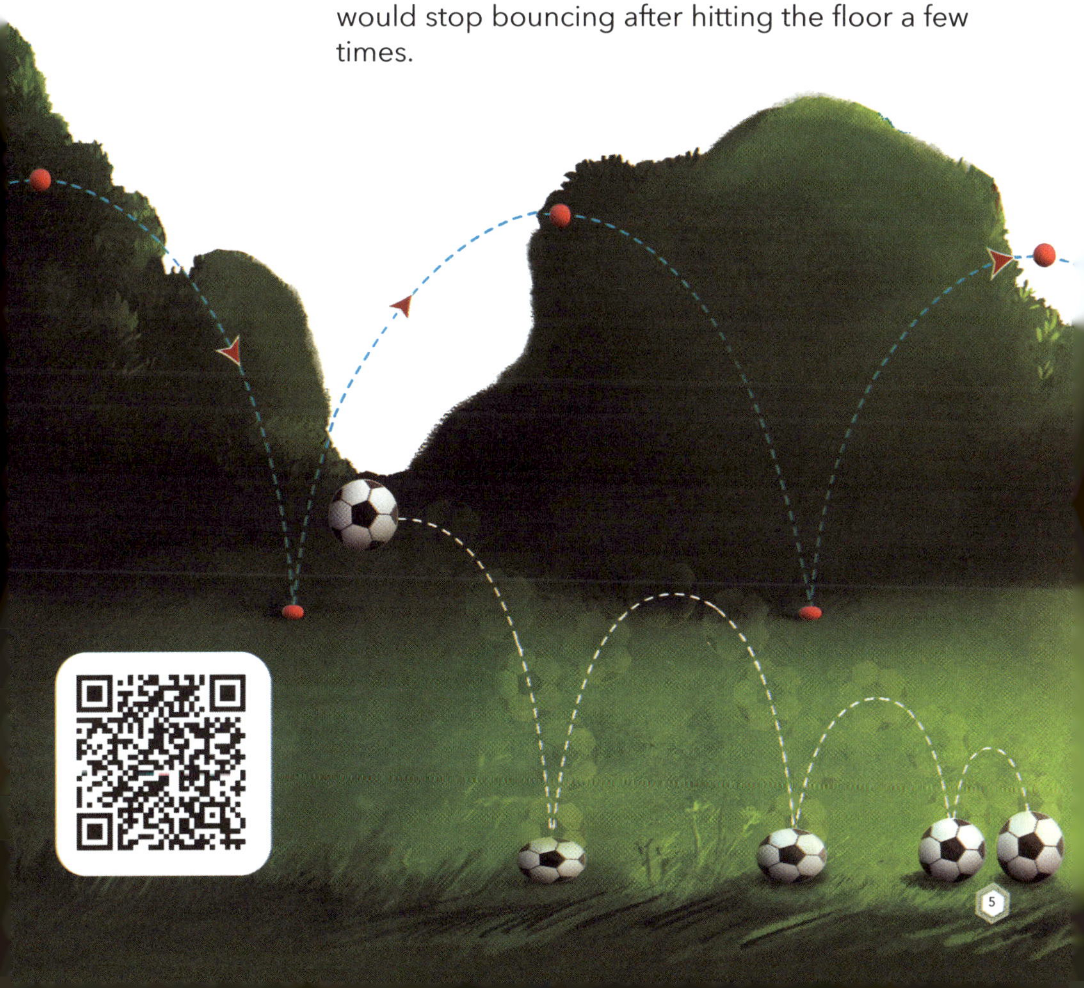

FUN FACTS

Different types of balls have different characteristics. For example, they can vary in size, thickness, weight and the amount of air that is needed to inflate them. All of these factors affect how the ball will bounce when it's thrown.

If you compare it with other balls, the super ball would probably be the best at bouncing. This is because it is very elastic and is able to maintain much of its height as

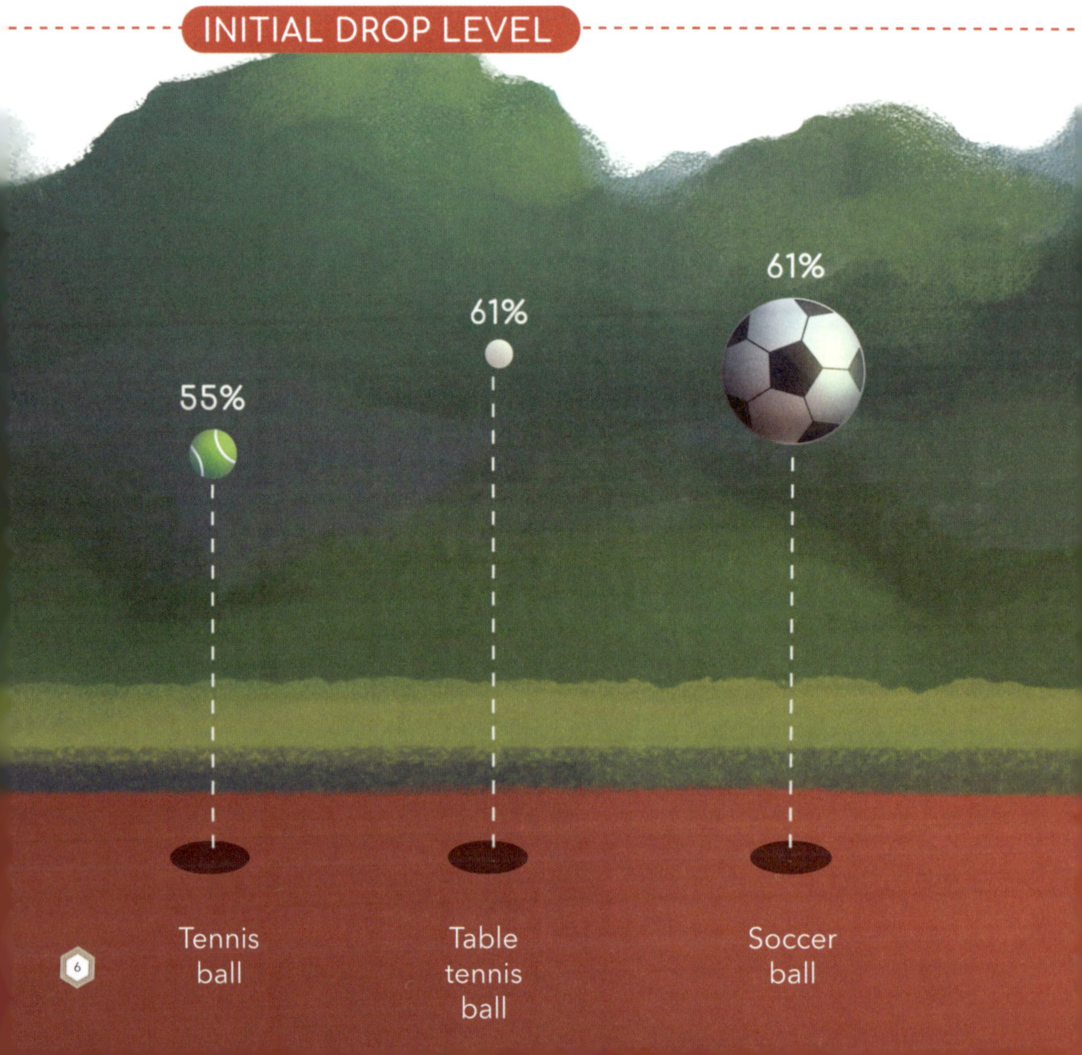

it bounces. While it's true that there are some other types of balls that would beat the super ball in a competition, those balls are not as easy to play with. For example, you could throw a steel ball onto a steel surface and it would bounce higher than the super ball.

But it's pretty hard for most people to find these materials. Meanwhile, a super ball can be thrown by anyone on any surface!

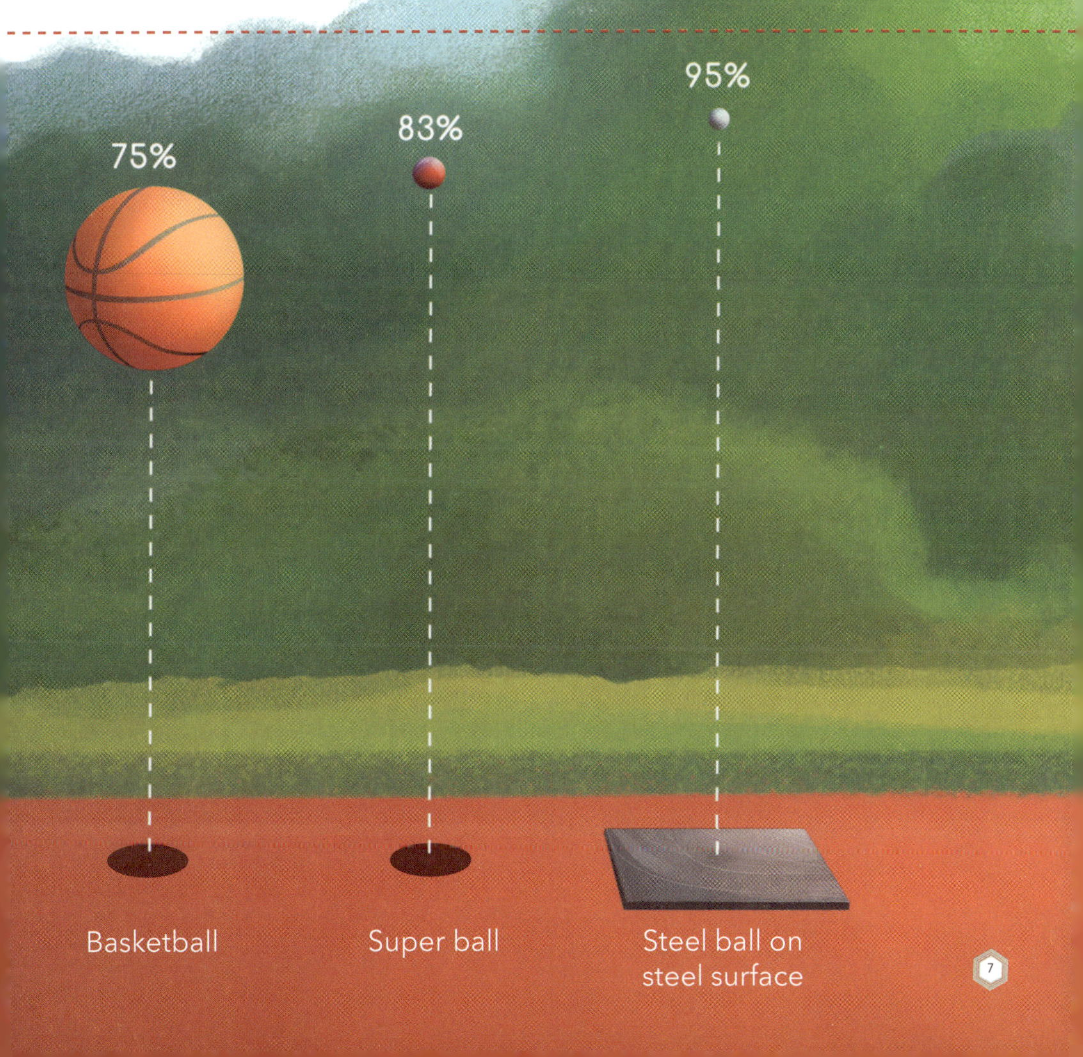

GRASP THE PHYSICS CONCEPT

Let's take a look at why the super ball bounces so well. To do this, let's familiarise ourselves with the concept of energy in physics.

Energy can be explained as the ability to do work. There are two types of energy: kinetic energy and potential energy.

The super ball has kinetic energy as a result of moving. The super ball's potential energy is stored energy that comes from factors such as its distance from the ground, whether it is compressed or stretched and so on.

The law of conservation of energy tells us that energy can't be created or destroyed; it can only be transferred from one type of energy to another. That means that the total amount of energy will stay constant, but the type of energy can change back and forth between kinetic energy and potential energy.

Kinetic and potential energies can be transferred back and forth in many different ways.

Here is one example: the energy a baseball player gains from eating breakfast is stored in her muscles. This energy can then be used to do work, such as swinging a baseball bat. In this case, the energy stored in the baseball player's muscles is an example of potential energy. The baseball player gives the ball kinetic energy when she swings the bat, sending the ball flying at high speed.

Let's look a little closer at the super ball to understand this idea. The super ball tries to hold on to as much energy as it can – that's how it can bounce as high as it does. But after it is thrown, the super ball loses some of its energy. For instance, with every bounce, the super ball will bounce a little lower due to the impact of friction.

What is friction, you ask? Well, as the ball moves through the air, it pushes air particles out of its way. As it hits the ground or bounces off a wall, the ball shakes and heats up a little. All of these things lead to energy losses (friction).

Any ball that is thrown will eventually stop moving due to the impact of friction, but the super ball is special because it is able to keep moving for a longer time than most other balls.

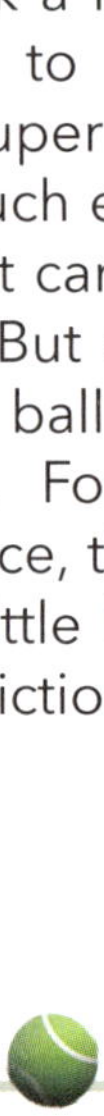

LEVEL UP PHYSICS AT PLAY

Now, let's see how this applies to the super ball: you throw the super ball, giving it kinetic energy, then the super ball flies into a wall and returns back to you. Let's take a closer look at what is going on.

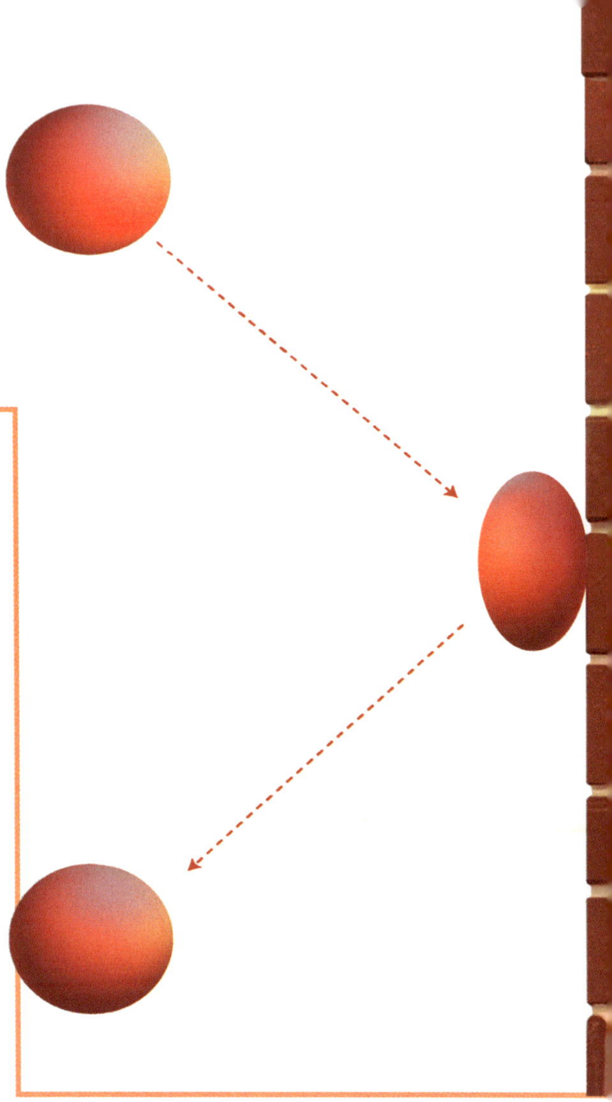

When the super ball hits the wall, it can't keep moving forward – the wall prevents that.

At this point, the kinetic energy will completely transform into potential energy. The ball hits the wall, and the force of the collision causes the ball to morph into an oval-like shape (as you see in the picture). But because the super ball is made up of a very rubbery and elastic material, it wants to return to its original shape.

In the process of changing back to its original round shape, the ball's potential energy is turned into kinetic energy, and it flies back from the wall.

The total energy remains the same at every stage of the ball's journey, it simply transforms from one type of energy to another, and back again.

BONUS LEVEL THE GALILEAN CANNON

Let's take a look at another excellent demonstration of the law of energy and momentum conservation: the Galilean cannon.

As you can see in the illustration, the Galilean cannon is made up of different sizes of balls that are stacked on top of one another.

To make your own "cannon" at home, I suggest you use very bouncy balls for the best result. Carefully stack the balls on top of one another, from smallest to largest, and then drop the stack of balls onto the floor. Watch what happens!

After hitting the floor, most of the energy is transferred to the top ball. This effect is the result of the law of energy and momentum conservation.

You can think of a ball's momentum as similar to its kinetic energy (they are related), but momentum also includes information about where the ball is flying to (direction).

The momentum and the energy from each of the balls concentrate in the ball sitting at the top of the stack. The top ball can gain so much energy that it bounces much higher than the balls were thrown – a bit like a cannon shooting a cannon ball!

YO-YO

WHAT'S THAT TOY?

The yo-yo is sometimes called "Maxwell's pendulum" by scientists, after James Clerk Maxwell who was a great Scottish physicist and mathematician.

The yo-yo can be described as a sort of cylinder that is attached to a string. Here is how it works: first, the string is wound up around the yoyo.

Then the yo-yo is released, and it drops to the floor. When it reaches the end of its string, it rebounds back towards your hand.

The yo-yo moves up and down again until it loses all of its energy. Unfortunately, the yo-yo's energy is lost quite quickly – that's why it's necessary to keep tugging the yo-yo upwards to keep it going.

LEVEL UP GRASP THE PHYSICS CONCEPT

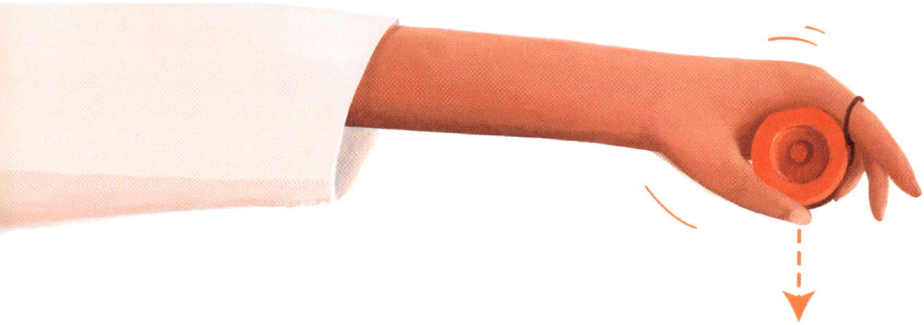

Now let's look at the physics behind the yo-yo. As you hold the yo-yo above the floor, you give it potential energy. The higher it is from the floor, the higher its potential energy. When you let it drop, the string unwinds and the yo-yo falls and spins, and its potential energy is turned into kinetic energy.

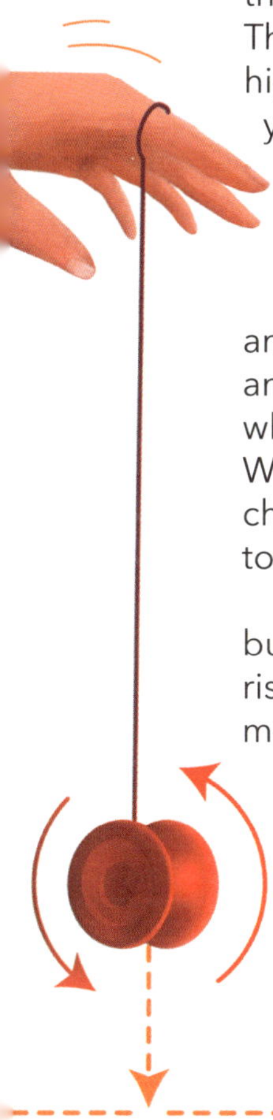

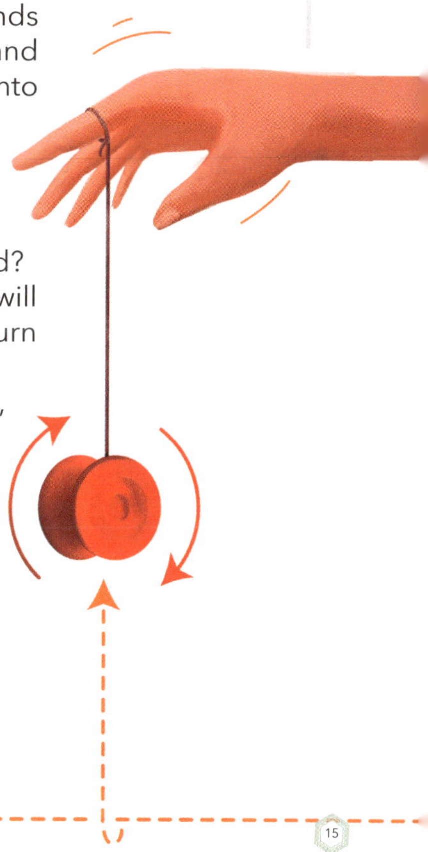

The longer you let the yo-yo fall and spin, the greater its velocity and rotation rate. But what happens when there is no string left to unwind? With nowhere left to fall, the yo-yo will change direction and slowly return towards your hand.

Now, it loses its speed and spin, but it gains height. As the yo-yo rises, it accumulates more and more potential energy.

BONUS LEVEL

WHAT A TIMELY TOY!

Did you know that you can use a yo-yo to measure time? To explain this, let me tell you about the ancient Egyptian pharaoh, Seti I.

Seti I ruled in the early 12th century BC. He was a pharaoh of the 19th Dynasty of Egypt, and the son of Ramesses I. During his rule, he worked on three great architecture projects, one of which was the Great Hypostyle Hall within the Karnak Temple complex. The hall included 134 sandstone columns.

As the construction of the columns neared its end, all that was left to do was to carve the hieroglyphics. Now, that might not sound like such a big deal to you, but Seti realised that a whole team of workers would need more than a month to finish a single wall! In order to plan the grand opening ceremony, Seti needed to find a way to estimate how long it would take to finish the project.

Seti typically measured time using an hourglass, which allowed him to keep track of time in approximately 10-minute periods. To measure an hour, he would have had to reset the hourglass 6 times. This measurement was not precise, and it didn't work well unless the time being measured was a multiple of 10.

For example, to measure 75 minutes the hourglass would run up to 5 minutes early or late. This would mean that when the hourglass suggested 75 minutes had passed, it might have actually been anywhere between 70 to 80 minutes. We could write this as "75 min ± 5 min".

Importantly, each time we repeated the measurements and added the results together, we would be even less sure of the true result.

If you knew 70 to 80 minutes had passed, and you measured two of these periods of time with the same error, the actual result could be between 140 to 160 minutes. That could mean your measurement was off by 20 minutes. Imagine the impact this would have if you wanted to measure months or years!

Returning to our story, Seti needed to know how long it would take to complete the hieroglyphics so that the grand opening ceremony could be planned.

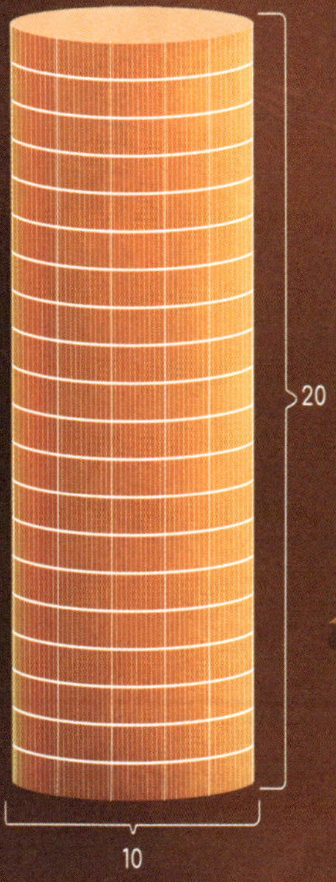

One column took a long time to finish, so Seti decided to focus his attention on a single layer of the column, amounting to 1/20th of the column itself. Because even a small layer of this size would take too long to practically measure, Seti decided to divide each layer into 10 sections. This was much easier to measure!

Seti was now able to record how long it took to finish one section, and then multiply the result by 10 to estimate how long the sculptors would need to complete the whole layer of the column.

He could then multiply the result by 20 to get the total time spent on the column. Seti found that one section of the column took 40 min ± 5 minutes to complete. Now all he needed to do was some math.

1 year = 365 days = 365 × 24 hour = 365 × 24 × 60 minutes = 525,600 minutes

* Egyptians used this device to add, subtract, multiply and divide.

LET'S CALCULATE

- (40 ± 5) mins × 10 = the time to complete one layer of the column.
- previous result × 20 = the time to complete a whole column.
- previous result × 120 = the time to finish all of the columns.

How many years does that equal?

According to this calculation, Seti had to wait about 22 months ± 3 months to finish the project! This small error of measurement – which started out as a 5-minute difference, either way – may have led to a 6-month difference in the estimated project completion date!

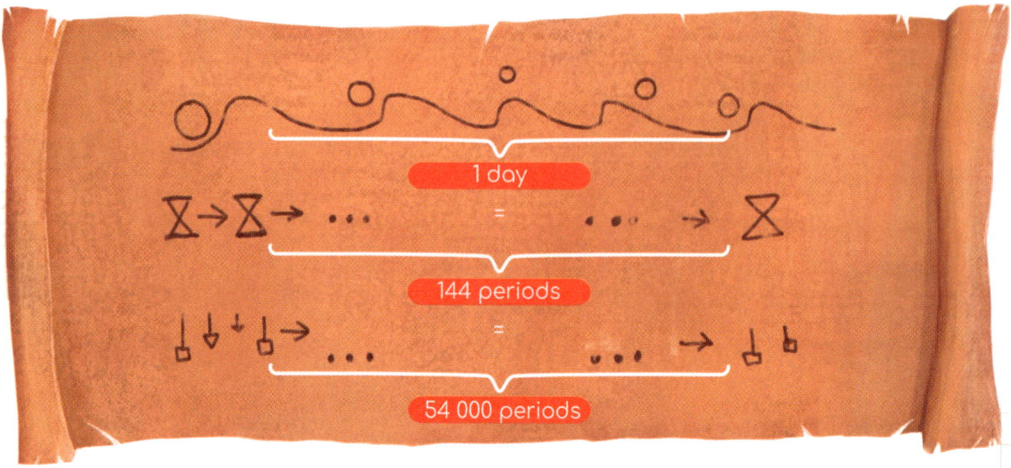

However, Seti had heard that it was possible to measure time using a pendulum. A pendulum is an object that swings back and forth repetitively, just like a yo-yo. Each cycle of the pendulum (that is, each time it swings back and forth) is called a "period". By measuring the period of a pendulum, we can calculate time.

For example, one day was equal to 144 periods of the hourglass that Seti had previously used. On the other hand, one day equalled 54,000 periods of his personal yo-yo. If he accidentally missed counting one period of the yo-yo, this would result in a much smaller error than it would if he missed one period of the hourglass.

Although Seti didn't know the period of his yo-yo, he could easily calibrate the yo-yo using his hourglass. To do this, he simply had to count the number of cycles his yo-yo could complete by the time the hourglass ran out of sand. His result: 400 cycles of the yo-yo were completed within the 10 minute period of his hourglass. Now he knew that each cycle of his yo-yo took 1.5 seconds.

Using his yo-yo as a timer, he found that each section of a column took 1680 cycles to complete, ± 40 cycles.

This meant that a single section of the column took 42 minutes ± 1 minute to finish. Now, let's figure out how long the whole project actually took!

LET'S CALCULATE

- (42 ± 1) mins × 10 = the time to complete one layer of the column.
- previous result × 20 = the time to complete a whole column.
- previous result × 120 = the time to finish all of the columns.

How many years is that?

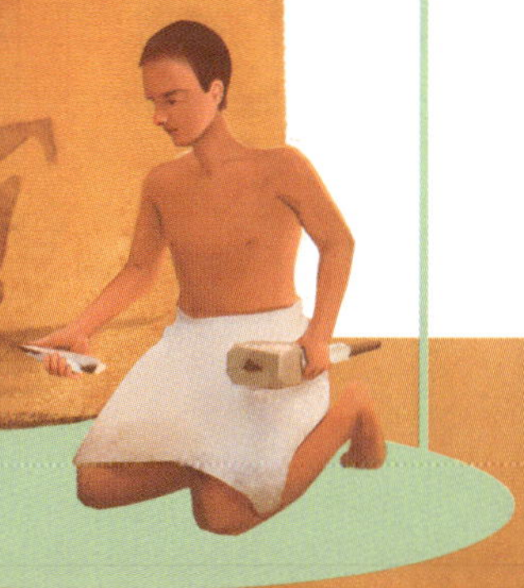

While it took quite a lot of work to improve his measurements, he was rewarded for his efforts. Seti was able to learn when to expect the temple to be finished – and now, if you've completed the calculation above, you'll know how long it took, too!

DARUMA DOLL

The Daruma doll is a traditional Japanese doll, which is seen as a symbol of luck.

If you set the Daruma doll down, it will always stand upright. You can try to push it, tilt it sideways, or even turn it upside down, but it will always return to its original position. To understand what is going on we need to understand a physics concept: the centre of mass, which is also referred to as the centre of gravity.

LEVEL UP

GRASP THE PHYSICS CONCEPT

The centre of mass is a point of balance. All objects, humans and animals, have a centre of mass. An object's centre of mass is influenced by its shape and weight. Some objects even have this centre of mass on their outside, e.g., doughnuts and bananas.

Let's look at the seesaw, which is a common sight to see in the playground: two objects are able to balance on a seesaw because their centre of mass rests above a pivot point. You can put anything on a seesaw and it will balance if the centre of mass is exactly above or below the pivot point.

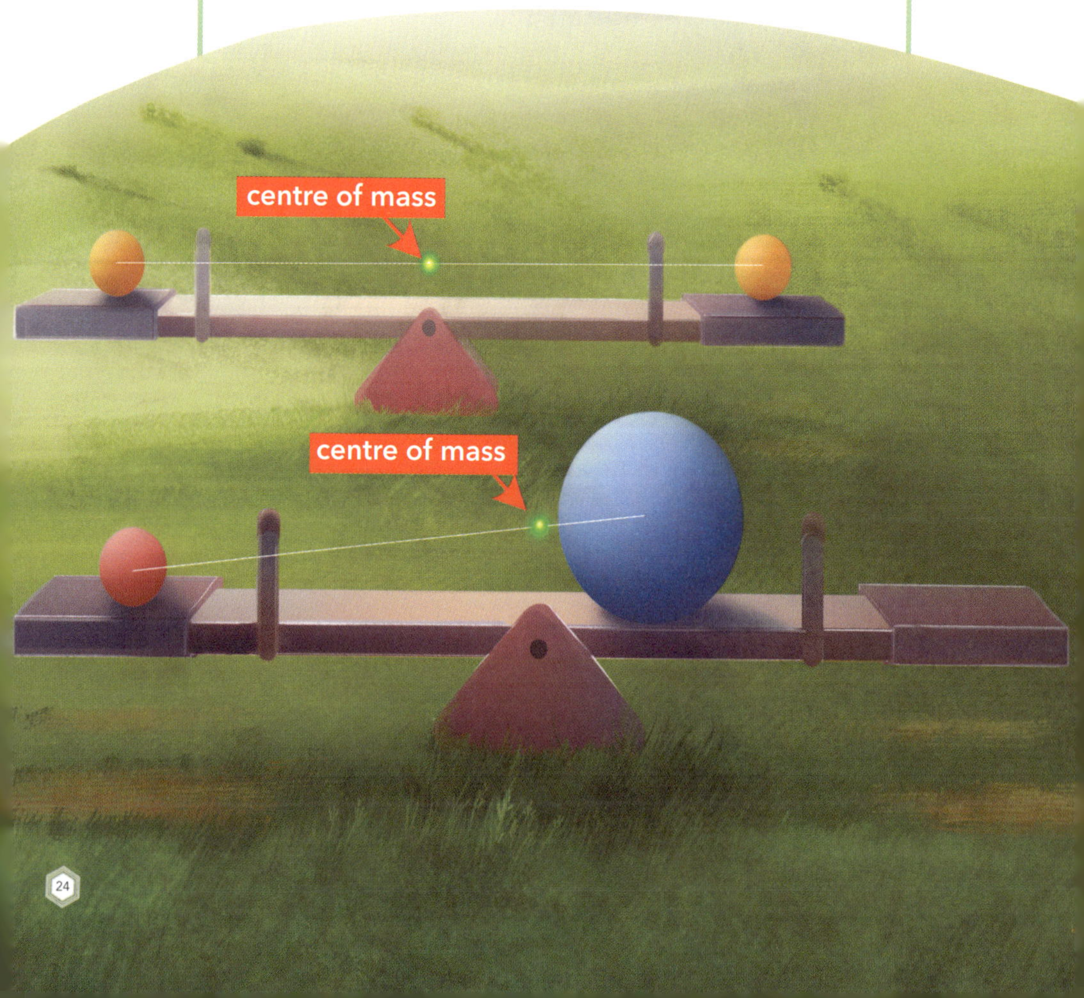

LET'S CHEW ON THIS!

You can often guess where an object's centre of mass is by looking at an object's shape.

Let's guess where the centre of mass is on a pizza. No matter how you rotate it, a round pizza will look the same. That means that its centre of mass also stays in the same place.

Now, where do you suppose the centre of mass will be? There is one single point that doesn't move, no matter how you rotate a pizza – its centre!

However, if you eat a slice, the position of the centre of mass changes. It is no longer in the middle of the pizza. Now the centre of mass shifts towards the heaviest part of the pizza.

BONUS LEVEL LEANING IN FROM HISTORY

Another great example to help us understand the centre of mass is the Leaning Tower of Pisa. This tower was built almost 200 years ago, and it is 55.86 metres high. Over time, the tower began to tilt because it was built on a soft, unstable foundation. Although it is tilted, it hasn't fallen over. Why is that?

If the tower leaned too far to one side, gravity would pull it downwards and it would fall over. If you look at the image, the tower would rotate (or fall) around the "R" point. The part of the tower which we have coloured red wants to pull the tower down. However, the much larger part we have highlighted in blue holds the tower and stabilises it.

Another way to see this is to think of the tower as an empty object with all of its mass concentrated in the centre of gravity (mass), which we have labeled "M". The tower will remain stable unless the "M" point shifts too close to the "R" point. Even with all of the tourists visiting the tower, their weight doesn't shift the "M" position any closer to the "R" point. This means that it is absolutely safe to visit the Leaning Tower of Pisa.

LEVEL UP

PHYSICS AT PLAY

Now that we understand a little more about the centre of mass, let's return to our Daruma doll. The toy's ability to remain upright, no matter how you push it, is the result of its form and the position of its centre of mass. The doll is roughly oval-shaped, and its centre of mass is shallow.

To understand why the doll resists being tilted, think of it as a solid, empty object with all of its weight concentrated in its centre of mass (which we have highlighted in the image as a green dot). The further you move the doll from its resting position, the higher the centre of mass is.

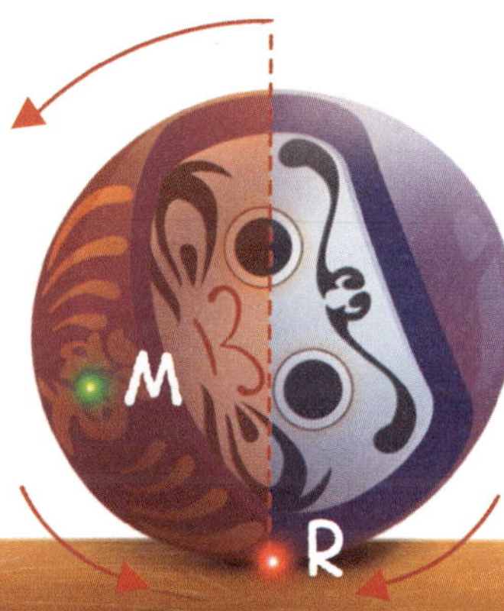

When this happens, the heavier part pulls the Daruma down, in an attempt to return it to its resting position and set it up straight. It is almost as though the centre of mass wants to be as low to the Earth as possible, and the Daruma doll tries to obey this wish.

HEAVY LIFTER

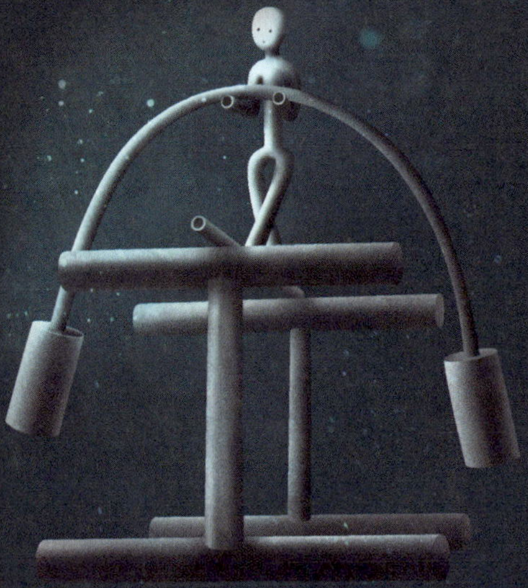

The heavy lifter toy is made up of two parts: the platform and the lifter (we'll call him Jack). Jack stands on a platform, but he is not glued to it. It's easy to tilt him on his platform.

If you move Jack a bit, he will come back to his starting place. Jack is pretty good at balancing, but he's not as stable as the Daruma doll we learned about in the last chapter. If you tilt him too much, he will fall. In his defence, unlike the Daruma doll, he also has to hold a dumbbell in his hands, which makes his work a little harder!

How exactly does he manage to balance and lift his dumbbell at the same time?

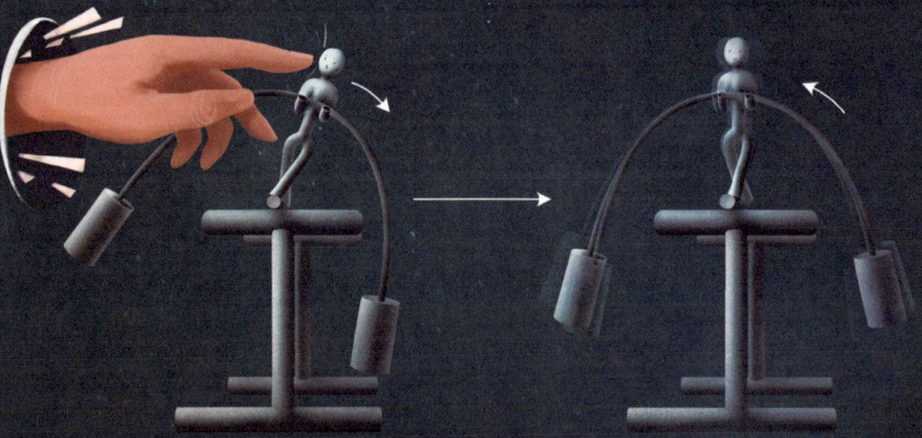

LEVEL UP GRASP THE PHYSICS CONCEPT

To understand how the heavy lifter works, we could think back to the Daruma doll chapter, and imagine Jack similarly as an empty object with all of his mass focused within his centre of mass. But there is something else we can learn here – a different explanation which involves another physics concept: torque.

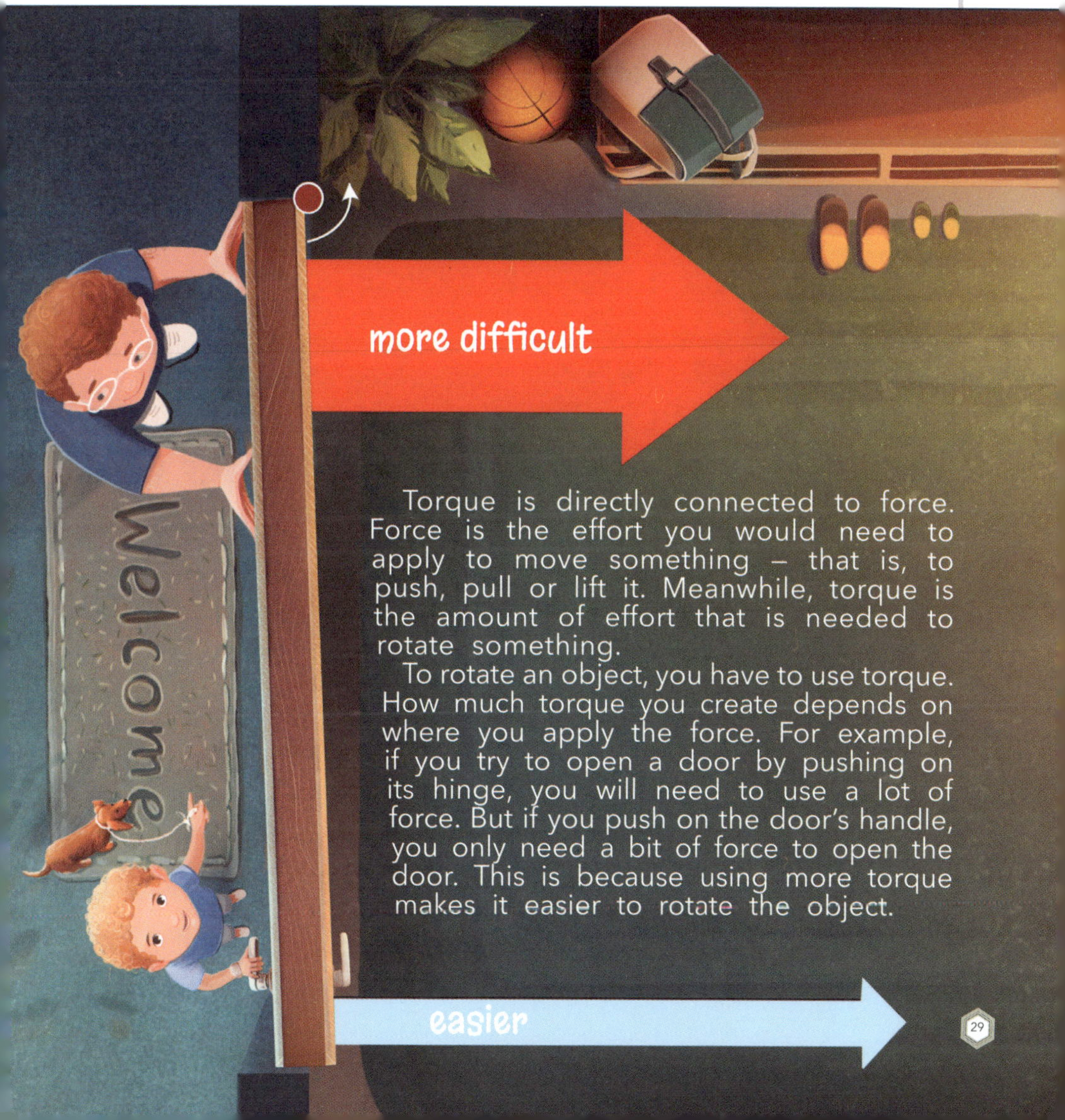

Torque is directly connected to force. Force is the effort you would need to apply to move something – that is, to push, pull or lift it. Meanwhile, torque is the amount of effort that is needed to rotate something.

To rotate an object, you have to use torque. How much torque you create depends on where you apply the force. For example, if you try to open a door by pushing on its hinge, you will need to use a lot of force. But if you push on the door's handle, you only need a bit of force to open the door. This is because using more torque makes it easier to rotate the object.

BONUS LEVEL

LET'S LIFT!

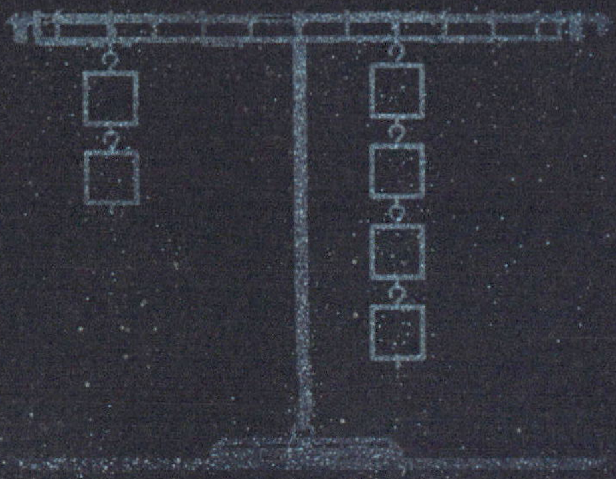

Another example of torque is the lever, which works like a seesaw: the further away from the pivot point that you apply force, the easier it is to lift things.

Just as a child can balance an adult on the seesaw, levers are used in construction to move heavy blocks, stones or other objects.

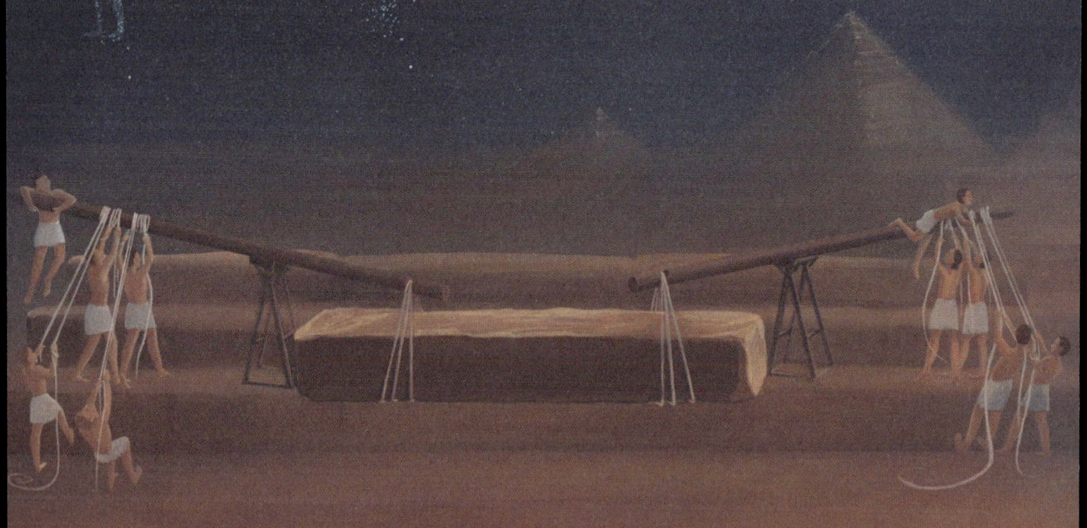

Archimedes of Syracuse was a Greek mathematician, physicist, engineer, inventor and astronomer. He made a significant contribution to our modern-day understanding of physics. Once he said that given a place to stand, he could lift the Earth. One way to think about this phrase is that you can lift heavy objects with little force but large torque. For that, you will need a long lever.

LEVEL UP PHYSICS AT PLAY

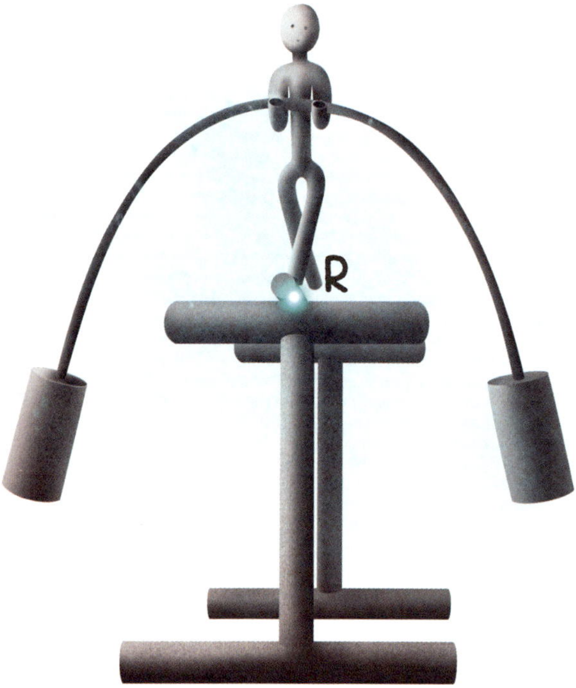

Let's go back to Jack and his dumbbell, Jack stands on a platform, at a point we will call "R". We can consider Jack and his dumbbell as an empty shell, with their combined mass concentrated in the centre of mass. But where is the centre of mass?

Jack, on his own, is light. The heaviest part of the toy would be the dumbbells. This means that the toy's centre of mass is somewhere between Jack's two dumbbells, slightly shifted upwards due to mass of Jack himself. If you look at the picture, you will see that the centre of mass is at the "M" point.

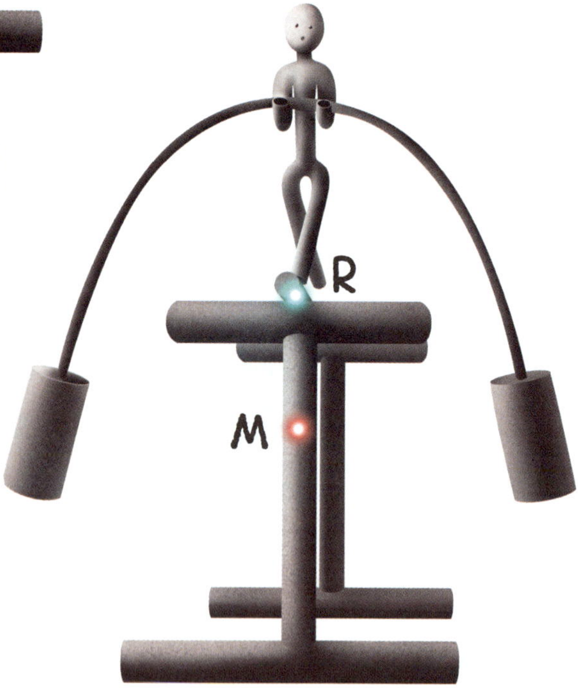

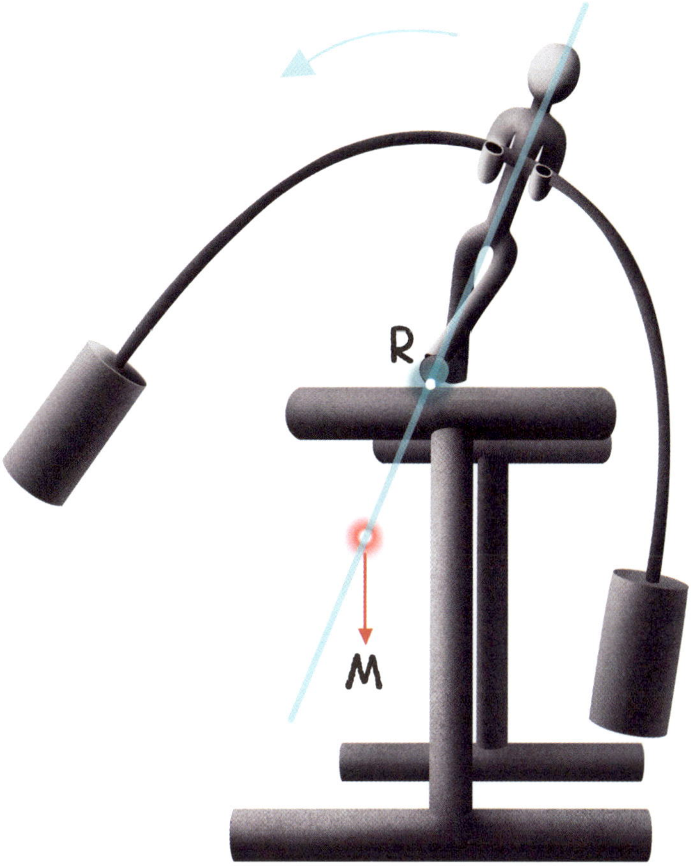

Whenever Jack moves, the centre of mass rises. If points "M" and "R" are not exactly above and below each other, gravity (force) creates torque. The gravitational torque rotates Jack back to his starting position. In other words, gravity pulls the centre of mass to the lowest possible position, just as it did in the case of the Daruma doll.

ASTROJAX

WHAT'S THAT TOY?

The Astrojax was invented by Larry Shaw in 1986. It's made up of three balls on a string, two of which are attached to each end of the string while the ball in the middle is free to move between the two. The way the middle ball is designed keeps the string from getting tangled up.

LEVEL UP

GRASP THE PHYSICS CONCEPT

In the last chapter, we learnt about torque, which is something that makes objects rotate. When torque is applied to an object, it gains angular momentum. This means that any rotating object (for example, a ball or the Astrojax) has angular momentum when it rotates.

Angular momentum tells us how exactly an object rotates. In physics, people use it to mathematically show important information about rotation.

A merry-go-round is a great object to help us understand rotational principles and angular momentum. Have you ever tried to pull yourself towards the centre, holding on tightly to avoid being thrown off the merry-go-round as it spun?

This force that you have to apply in order to stay on a merry-go-round as it spins is called centrifugal force.

How much force is needed to stay on the merry-go-round will change depending on how fast the merry-go-round is rotating, and how far you are from the merry-go-round's centre. This force also changes depending on your mass. Just try standing on a spinning merry-go-round while wearing a heavy backpack, and you'll see it's much harder to hold on!

LEVEL UP GRASP THE PHYSICS CONCEPT

I once saw a group of children playing on a merry-go-round, spinning super fast! Here is what happened:

First, each child stood at the edge of the merry-go-round. Then, one of the parents spun the merry-go-round as fast as he or she could.

At that point, all of the children moved to the centre and the merry-go-round began to spin (or rotate) much faster.

Now here's the physics behind the phenomenon, which is called "the law of conservation of angular momentum". This law tells us that, as each child (child's mass) on the merry-go-round moves closer to the axis of rotation, the merry-go-round will rotate more quickly.

FUN FACTS

PHYSICS IN FIGURE SKATING

Figure skaters use the law of conservation of angular momentum to spin themselves incredibly quickly. You may have seen this: first, the skater spins with hands outstretched. Then, the skater clasps his hands and one leg close to his body, increasing his rotation frequency by two to three times. This is due to the very same effect that the children used on the merry-go-round.

BONUS LEVEL CAN YOU DO THIS?

Now, let's go back to the Astrojax. There are countless tricks you could learn and perform with the Astrojax – I'll give you some examples below. But, of course, you can (and should!) invent your own tricks, improve your coordination and get a better sense of angular momentum by playing with the Astrojax.

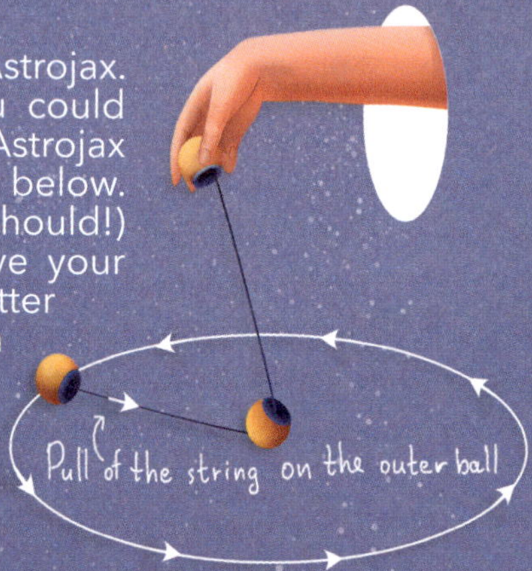

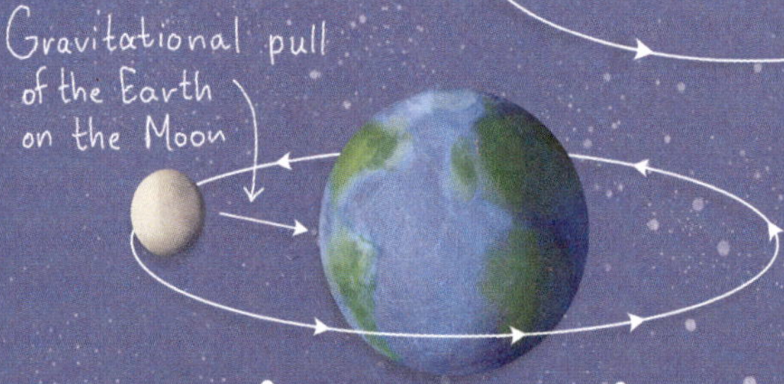

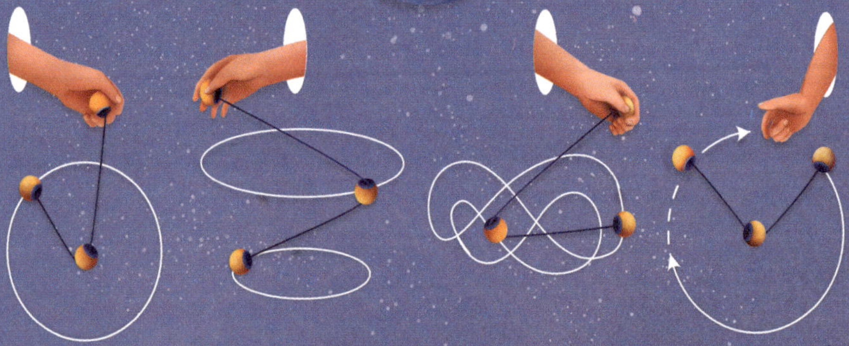

vertical orbits   horizontal orbits   butterfly   switch

To get a practical sense of centrifugal force and gravitational rotation, try holding the Astrojax's first ball in your hand while attempting to keep the second ball from moving, all while making the third ball rotate around the second one. This mimics the rotation of the moon!

SPINNING TOP

WHAT'S THAT TOY?

The spinning top is one of the oldest toys in the world. In fact, the lessons we've learnt from this simple toy have helped us to develop sophisticated modern technologies such as navigation systems!

The simplest version of the spinning top consists of two parts – the spindle and the disc. To launch the spinning top, you simply hold it by the spindle, twist it with your fingers and drop it on the table. It will stand and spin for a while before slowing down and toppling over.

There are dozens of versions of the spinning top from all over the world. For example, Russia has the *yule* or *qubar*, while the Jewish culture has the dreidel, Latin America has the *trompo*, and then there is Sakai's paper clip spinner that was invented in Japan.

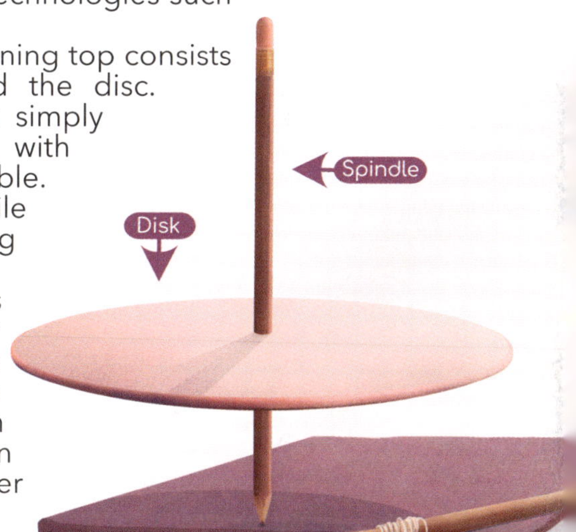

If you have a spinning top of your own, try balancing it on its spindle without spinning. You will notice that it falls over almost immediately. That's because gravity acts on the top and pulls it towards the Earth. Yet, if you give the top a spin before you put it down, it can stand upright for around a minute. How does the action of spinning help the top to defy gravity and avoid falling over?

When gravity tries to tilt the spin top, say to the right, gravity makes point "A" move towards the bottom while point "B" moves to the top. In other words, gravity gives a small vertical velocity with different directions to both ends. If the spinning top rotates very quickly, this contribution from gravity just slightly changes the total velocity at that points.

In a sense, rotation makes an object more stable. This is a very important point to remember, so we will return to it later.

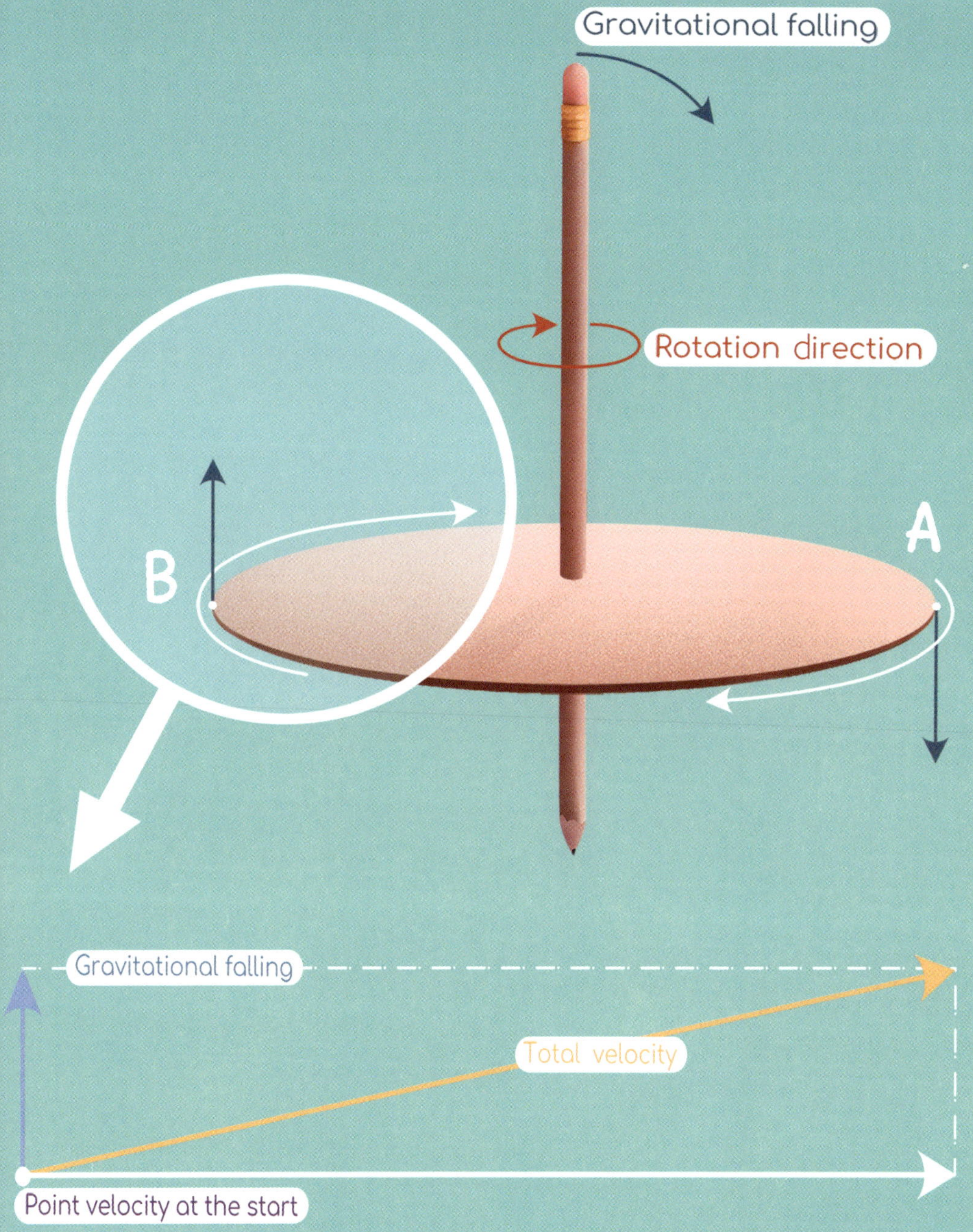
Gravitational falling
Rotation direction
A
B
Gravitational falling
Total velocity
Point velocity at the start

LEVEL UP GRASP THE PHYSICS CONCEPT

You'll notice the spinning top moves as it spins. Slow circle-like movements (see the illustration) are called "the precession". Precession refers to the way the spinning top moves when its incline stays constant.

In addition, when the top is spinning, it also wobbles. This wobble is called "the nutation". We can notice the wobble, or the nutation, at the beginning of the spinning top's rotation and also at the very end.

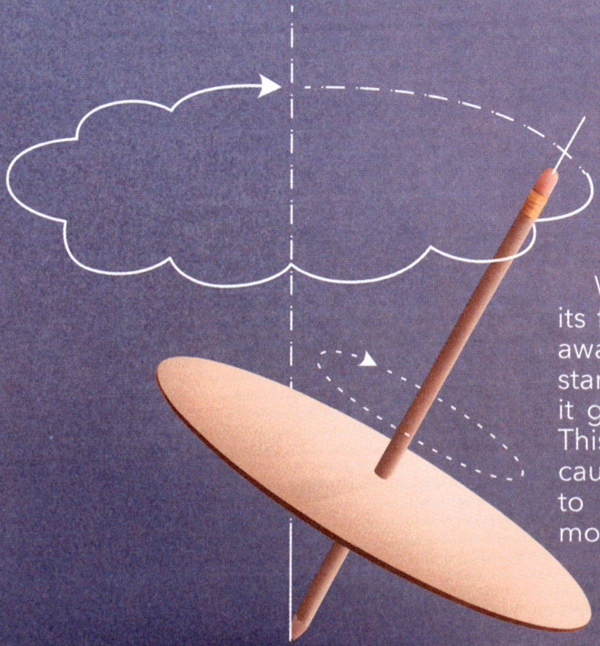

When the top is spinning its fastest, the wobble goes away. However, when the top starts spinning more slowly, it gets increasingly wobbly. This wobble eventually causes the spinning top to hit the table and stop moving.

LEVEL UP PHYSICS AT PLAY

You can create a homemade version of the spinning top using a pen. The pen acts as the top's axis of rotation.

For the first activity, find a piece of paper and spin your homemade spinning top on it.

Looking at the path that is traced, you will notice that the pen (or axis) has drawn some big circles and some smaller ones. The big circles show the precession, while the small ones are the result of the nutation, or the wobble.

You can actually find out how fast the top is spinning by looking at the path that is traced and using a timer. Count the number of small circles that are drawn per second – this is the spinning frequency.

This next activity will give you a sense of how the gyroscope (a cousin of the spinning top) is used for navigation. Take a solid surface, such as a tray or a cutting board, and set the top spinning on it. Now rotate the surface any way you wish – even on an angle (or slope). You should notice that the top will keep spinning straight and that it continues to rotate vertically, regardless of the surface tilt. This effect makes the navigation of planes, rockets and submarines possible!

Let's push our experiment a little further. Toss the spinning top into the air. You'll notice that the spinning top continues to rotate and stays straight, just as it did before, even while it's in the air! Its rotation gives it stability.

People make various objects rotate in order to stabilise them, for example, shells and bullets, satellites and rockets. The flying bullet makes between 1,000 to 4,000 rotations per second, and like the spinning top, it also experiences nutation and precession.

FUN FACTS

A JUGGLING ACT

For the last activity, you will need a bicycle wheel. Tie it to a rope and spin the wheel. This will cause the bicycle wheel to behave in a very unpredictable way. If it spins fast enough, eventually the wheel will turn on its side. This is due to the effect of gyroscopic precession.

Jugglers often make use of rotation in their tricks. Because a rotating object is stable, it is easy to predict where and how it will fall. This means that whatever object the juggler throws into the air, he or she will know how and where to safely catch it.

BONUS LEVEL

THE FINAL CHALLENGE!

One final suggestion: try creating a spinning top battleground! First, you'll need some spinning tops. Try to make your own using plasticine, gluc or other crafting materials you might have in your home. If you would like some tips, search the internet for designs. Next, you'll need an arena. You can create four borders for the arena, using books, furniture or anything else you can think of. Finally, get some friends together and set your tops spinning in the arena. You can compete with one another to see who has the best spinning top design!

EULER'S DISK

WHAT'S THAT TOY?

Back in the 19th century, mathematicians tried to understand and solve a variety of problems related to the behaviour of different objects. One of these problems was to understand what was going on when a solid object was rolling, spinning or otherwise moving on different kinds of surfaces.

Leonard Euler was one of the most famous mathematicians who significantly contributed to our understanding of these problems. The toy we will examine in this chapter is named after this great scientist.

We've all seen what happens when a coin falls on the table. But have you ever paid attention to the sound it makes? If you have, you might have noticed that the sound of a spinning coin gets louder and louder before the coin eventually stops moving. This effect is easier to notice if you toss a coin onto a metallic surface.

Joseph Bendik invented the toy known as Euler's Disk in the late 20th century. It is a flat disc made of highly polished chrome steel. It has a diameter of 3 inches and it is half an inch deep. We can use this disc to examine the spinning coin effect.

When I first saw the disc in motion, I was amazed at how it could keep spinning for up to three minutes when dropped onto a slightly concave mirror. That is a pretty impressive feat!

More significantly, the sound of Euler's Disk startled me. It got louder and louder, until it almost whistled!

In scientific terms, we would say that the sound's frequency increased significantly over time. But what is frequency, and why do we need it?

LEVEL UP GRASP THE PHYSICS CONCEPT

We can describe events that repeat themselves either by using period or frequency. Period is better used when describing rare events, such as the moon's phases or seasons. Frequency is best used with frequent events such as the movements of a yo-yo, the rotation of a wheel or the pitch of a sound. The greek letter ω (omega) is used to represent frequency. ω is a number that tells us how many times something happens per second.

LET'S CALCULATE

As an example, let's calculate the ω of a car tire's rotation. Here is how we'll do it: First, we need some data. The car's speedometer shows us the car is moving 108 kilometres per hour. It's also important for us to know that the diameter of each wheel is 48 cm.

Next, we need to figure out how many times the wheel must turn in order to travel a certain distance – let's say the distance is 30 metres. We'll divide this by the number of seconds a car travelling at a given velocity would need to move that distance.

The following calculation shows us that the velocity of the car is 30 metres per second:

$$V = 108 \frac{km}{hr} = 108 \frac{1000\ m}{60 \cdot 60\, s} = 30 \frac{m}{s}$$

So, now we know that the car's wheel travels 30 metres per second. How many rotations does it make within that second? With each rotation the wheel will move as far as the length of its tire, so it's important for us to figure out the length of the tire:

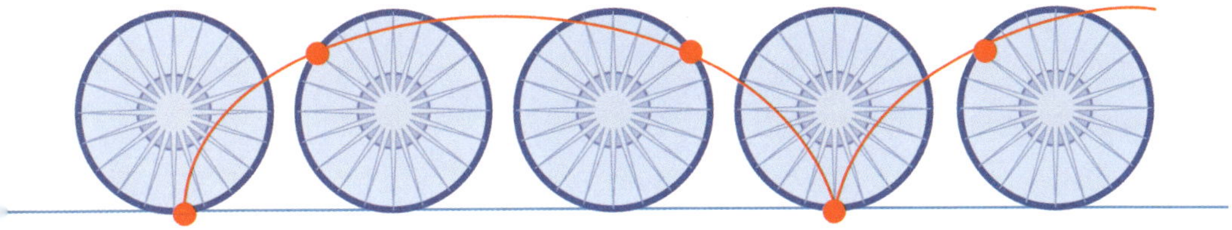

The length of a circle is equal to its diameter multiplied by a special number, known as π. By definition, π is the ratio of a circle's length (or circumference) to its diameter. This ratio is the same for all circles.

I challenge you to measure this on your own, using circles of different sizes! (Don't forget, however, that there is always some error of measurement; this means that the number you measure will be close to π).

Using the above information, we can perform a calculation: to show us that, in this case, the length of our wheel is:

LET'S CALCULATE

$$L = 2\pi R = \pi D, \quad \pi \approx 3.14$$

$$D = 47.8 \text{ cm} \quad L = \pi D \approx 150 \text{ cm} = 1{,}5 \text{ m}$$

Now we know that one rotation of the wheel means the car has travelled 1.5 metres. After 20 rotations the car has travelled 30 metres. Comparing the numbers above, we see that this wheel makes 20 rotations per second. Congratulations! We've gotten our answer: the wheel's frequency is 20 rotations per second.

One last point: frequency is measured in Hz. This unit was named after Heinrich Rudolf Hertz, who was the first person to prove the existence of electromagnetic waves. We can convert our wheel's frequency in Hz. If an event happens once per second, its frequency is 1 Hz. Our wheel makes 20 rotations per second, therefore its frequency equals 20 Hz.

LEVEL UP

PHYSICS AT PLAY

When you spin Euler's Disk, you give it energy and angular momentum. The slope of the disc depends on its potential energy, and the spinning motion depends on its kinetic energy and angular momentum.

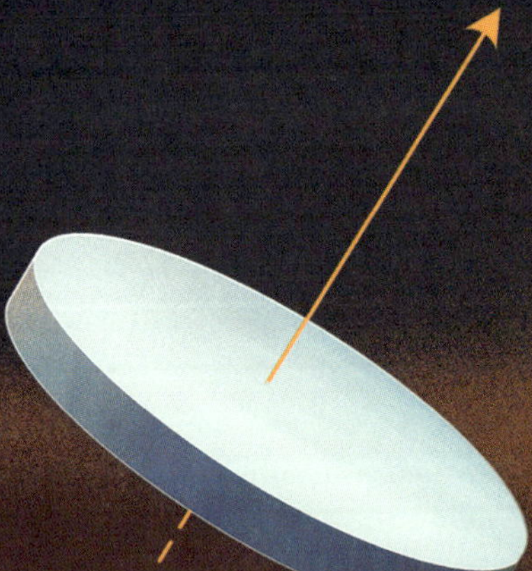

Over time, friction steals some of the kinetic energy away from the disc. Euler's Disk's potential energy makes up for this loss of kinetic energy. As a result, the angle of the Euler's Disk will decrease as it spins.

As the angle is reduced, the frequency of the precession (or rotation) increases rapidly. This rapid increase in frequency is a result of the law of conservation of angular momentum.

We can use here a similar idea to the rotation of a merry-go-round: as the slope decreases, the disc mass moves closer to its axis of rotation. This makes it spin faster, just like the kids on the merry-go-round made it go faster when they gathered at the axis-of-rotation. When the disc is so tilted that it's almost laying flat, it is incredibly close to its axis of rotation – it rotates superfast!

The fast oscillation (rotation) of the disc pushes away the air near to it. This fact, together with the vibrations of the disc and its surface produces the sound that you and I hear.

TIPPE-TOP

WHAT'S THAT TOY?

The tippe-top goes by many names, including the flip-top, the Chinese spinner and Thomson's spinner. It is a spinning top that is shaped like a mushroom. The "cap", or sphere, of this mushroom-shaped spinning top shifts the toy's centre of mass downwards. The centre of mass (point "M" in the illustration) is lower than the geometrical centre of the sphere (point "G"). Just like the regular spinning top, when the tippe-top is in motion, it rotates around two axes. See the illustration for more detail.

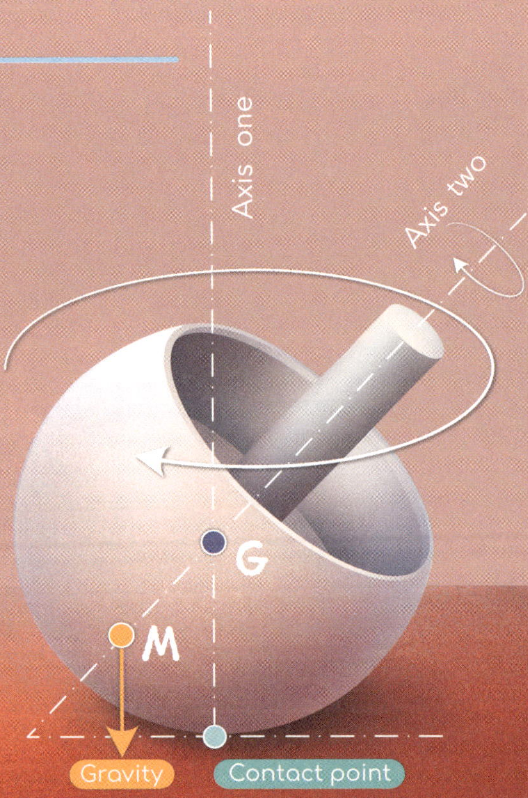

LEVEL UP

PHYSICS AT PLAY

If you spin a tippe-top and place it on a surface, you will see something incredible! First, the tippe-top will gradually lean over to one side until it's horizontal, and then it will stand upside down on its leg! This shift in position happens as a result of the rotation of the tippe top, which forces the sphere upwards.

To explain the scientific reasons for the remarkable action of the tippe-top would be too complicated and mathematical for this book. Instead, I'd like to focus on three interesting points:

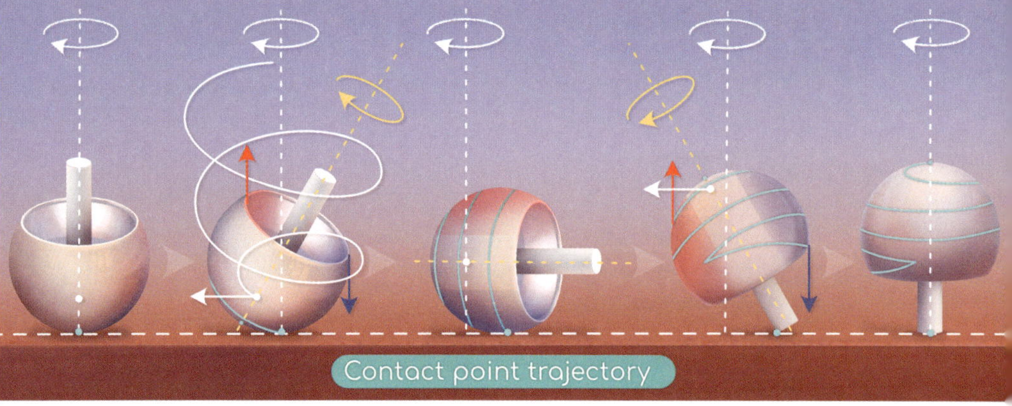

Firstly, the tippe-top is able to flip and then stabilise itself as it spins due to friction torque. Without friction, the tippe-top would not be able to stand on its leg.

Secondly, just like the common spinning top, the tippe-top has both precession and nutation, which you can see after it flips onto its leg.

The third and most surprising point has to do with the rotation of the tippe-top. At first, as it spins, the toy's sphere is in contact with the surface. As we've learnt, however, the tippe-top eventually flips upside down at which point its leg is in contact with the surface.

There is a specific moment in the middle of this move – when the toy is exactly horizontal – that it stops spinning, then spins in the opposite direction and finally stands on its leg.

That's all we'll say about the tippe-top. But remember, the physics of gyroscopes, spinning tops and rotating objects is very rich. Making even the smallest modification to these toys can dramatically change their behaviour. So, by all means, experiment and amaze your friends and family with your discoveries!

DYNABEE

WHAT'S THAT TOY?

The Dynabee looks like a ball within a shell – but it's not just a ball, it's actually a spinning top! People use the Dynabee as an exercise tool to train their wrists.

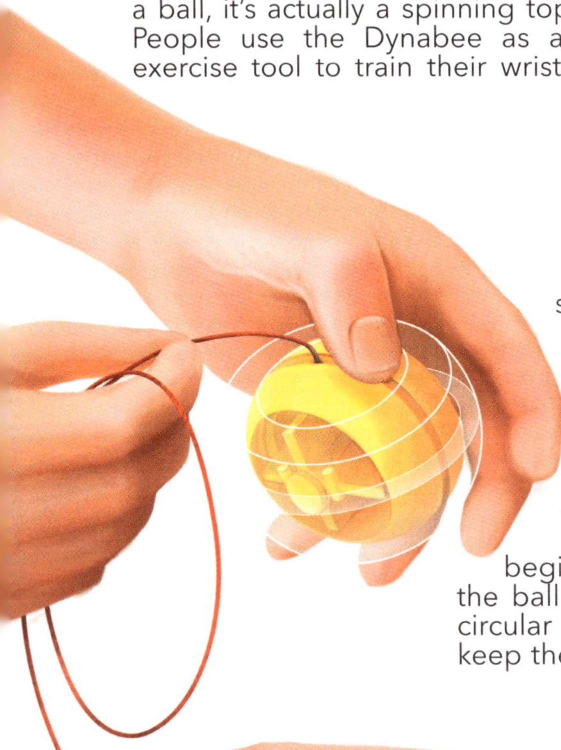

You can get the Dynabee to start spinning by using a string: insert the stiff end of the string into the hole in the yellow ball, then rotate the ball to wrap the string around it. Once the string is wrapped around the ball, pull the string out as fast as you can!

You will notice the ball begins to rotate quickly. Now grip the ball with your hand and make small circular motions with your wrist to keep the Dynabee spinning.

LEVEL UP UNDERSTANDING GYROSCOPES

The foundation of the Dynabee is a gyroscope. In this book, we will only take a brief look at the gyroscope.

The gyroscope is a spinning top mounted within three frames (known as "gimbals"), which allow it to rotate freely.

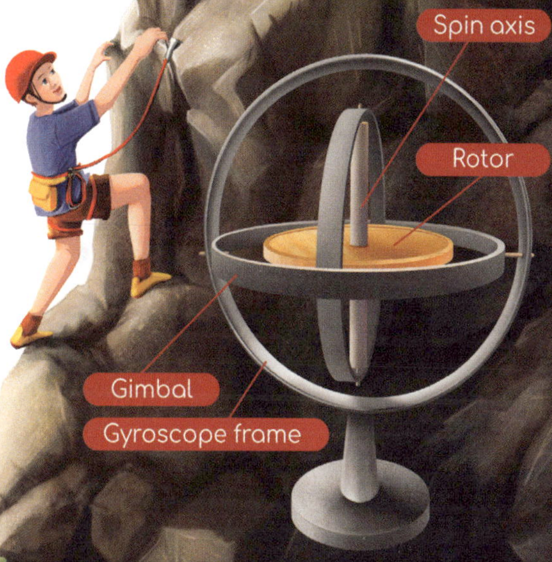

When I say that it can freely rotate, I mean that if you spin the central disc and move the gyroscope by its outer handle, the spinning disk won't react. The angle the disc is spinning at will stay constant. That is why gyroscopes are so important to sailors and pilots, for example, to help them navigate.

BONUS LEVEL

John Serson invented the first known device similar to a gyroscope, (the "Whirling Speculum" or "Serson's Speculum") in 1743. Sailors used it to locate the horizon in foggy or misty conditions.

As a ship or an airplane travels, it will shake, rise up and down, move back and forth, and so on. This can make it difficult to keep a steady course. However, because a gyroscope will keep a steady angle, it's easier to find out the ship or airplane's true angle in space.

How could a submarine navigate through the oceans without using similar device? Even the tiniest error in the submarine's direction, caused by waves, could cause it to go off-course by hundreds of kilometres in one single day!

FUN FACTS

Over time, with the development of electricity and electric motors, it became possible for a gyroscope to work for much longer periods of time. This led to the creation of very complex devices such as gyrocompasses.

Later, the military importance of such technologies led to the emergence of an entire industry based on gyroscopes. This industry has led to great advances in air and naval transport. The existence of gyroscopes has even made it possible for humans to travel into space! The development of the gyroscope has been invaluable to the advancement of human technologies.

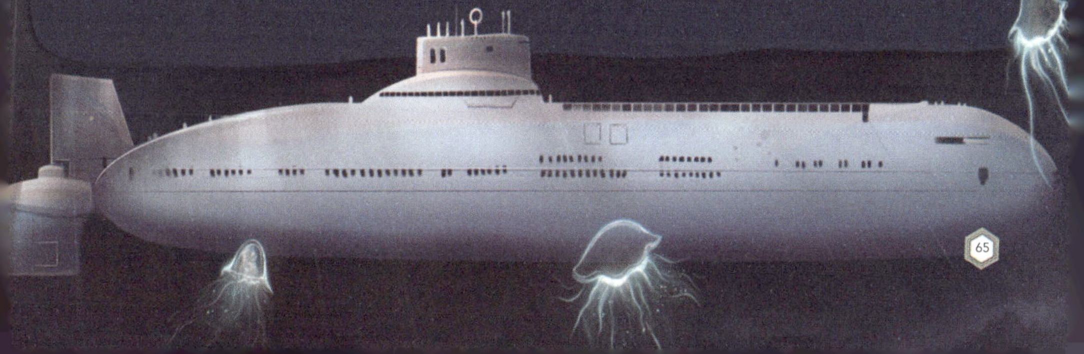

BONUS LEVEL

CAN YOU DO THIS?

So, as we learnt in the beginning of this chapter, the Dynabee has a gyroscope in its centre. By rotating your wrist while holding the Dynabee, you can make this gyroscope spin faster and faster – some people can even make it rotate 10,000 times per minute!

How is it used to train the wrists? Well, in order to turn the Dynabee while it is in motion, you'll need to use a surprising amount of muscle. This toy shows us that turning even very small and light objects while they are rotating requires a lot of effort! The Dynabee is a fun and useful tool which not only trains your wrists, but also clearly demonstrates that rotation provides stability.

RATTLEBACK

WHAT'S THAT TOY?

The rattleback was probably inspired by an ancient tool known as the "adze" or the "Celtic stone". The tip of this tool behaved very oddly when it was spun. Somehow, it seemed to move differently if it was spun to the right (clockwise) versus the left (counterclockwise), and it clearly preferred one direction over the other. The rattleback behaves in a similar way.

The rattleback looks a bit like an oval with a convex bottom and a flat top. Its strange spinning behaviour is the result of two weights, which are arranged on top of the object (see the picture for details). These weights cause the rattleback to rock back and forth when it spins, and that is the secret of its strange behaviour.

LEVEL UP PHYSICS AT PLAY

The rattleback spins very well in one direction. For example, this version spins best to the left:

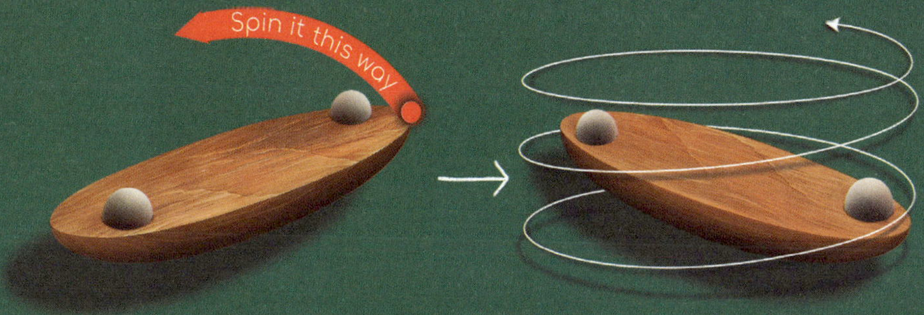

However, if you try to spin it the other way you'll see it does something very strange: first, it starts to shake, and then it stops rotating and begins to spin in the opposite direction. It seems as though the rattleback has a favourite path to take! How can this be?

LEVEL UP

GRASP THE PHYSICS CONCEPT

There is an important force at play which creates the torque that allows the rattleback to rock: friction. Without friction, the toy would spin equally well to the left or to the right. You can see this for yourself: place the rattleback onto an oiled surface, and try spinning it in either direction. Watch as it spins well, no matter which way you rotate it!

Friction torque causes the rattleback to rock and then to spin in the "right" direction. If you spin the rattleback in the "wrong" direction, the rocking motions will become exaggerated and quickly stop the toy from spinning.

The bigger the rocking motions, the easier it will be for the rattleback to resist turning in the "wrong" direction. The best rattleback toys will be able to make very large rocking movements – that is the most important detail in the toy's design.

To see how important the rocking motion is, try the following experiment: place the rattleback on a flat surface and press down on one of its ends. You'll see that it begins rocking and then starts spinning in the "right" direction.

KITE

WHAT'S THAT TOY?

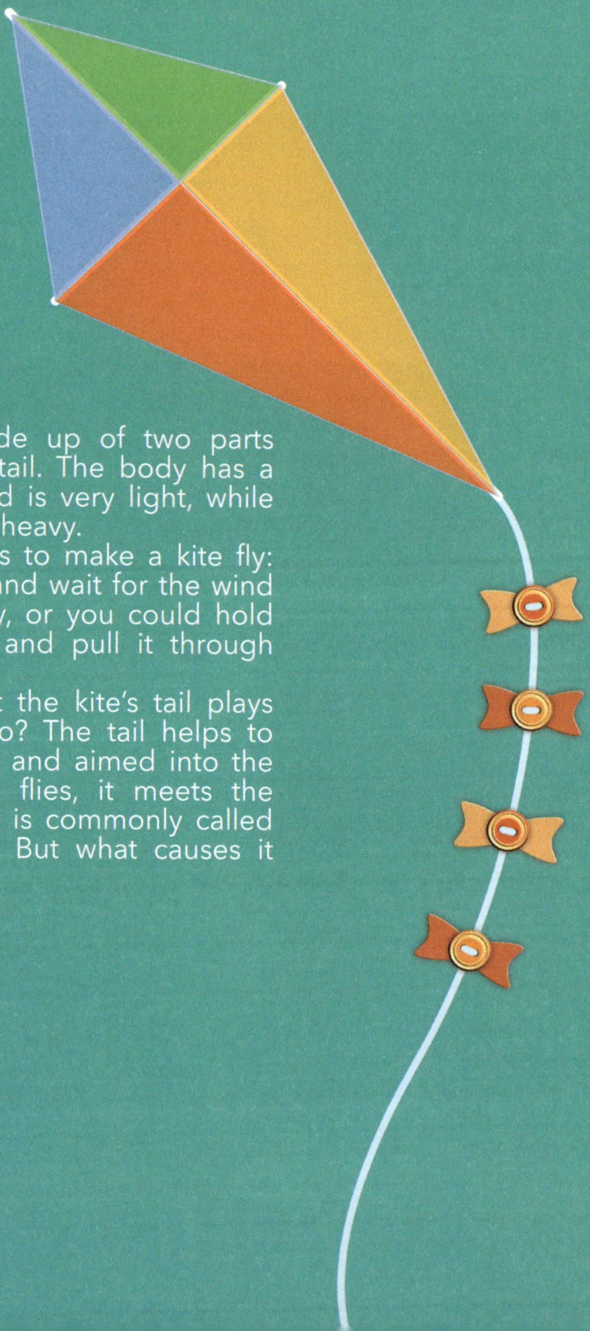

A simple kite is made up of two parts – the body and the tail. The body has a large surface area and is very light, while the tail is small but heavy.

There are two ways to make a kite fly: you might stand still and wait for the wind to carry the kite away, or you could hold the kite by its nose and pull it through the air as you run.

Did you know that the kite's tail plays an important role, too? The tail helps to keep the body stable and aimed into the wind. When the kite flies, it meets the wind at an angle that is commonly called the "angle of attack". But what causes it to fly?

LEVEL UP GRASP THE PHYSICS CONCEPT

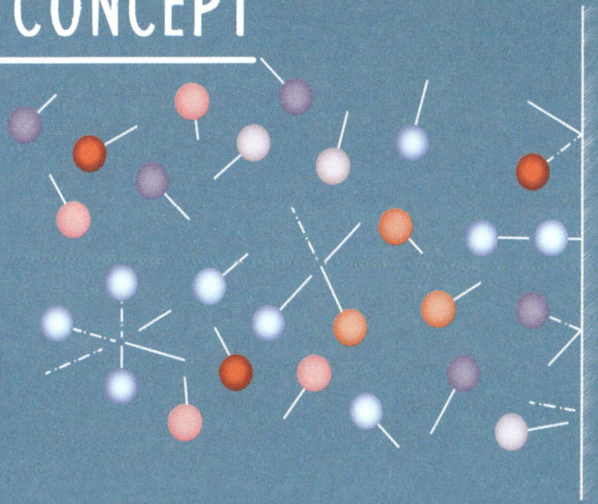

The air around us is made up of a countless number of particles. What are particles? You might think of them as tiny balls that are invisible to the naked eye.

Particles fly around, hitting objects and other particles as they go. As a particle hits other objects, it pushes them away, creating pressure. Usually, we are not pushed around by it, because it's acting on us from all directions. Imagine being in a crowded bus, with the other passengers bumping you from all around; you don't actually move anywhere, you're just a little squished!

Something dramatically different happens when a lot of air particles move together along the same direction: wind. Sometimes the pressure generated by the wind is so strong that it can break trees and demolish buildings!

LEVEL UP PHYSICS AT PLAY

A similar thing happens with our kite. A large number of air particles that are moving in the same direction (the wind) eventually collide with our kite. When this happens, the particles bounce off of it, pushing it. When the particles change their direction upon colliding with the kite's body, this creates the pressure that lifts the kite up into the sky. This also makes you feel some resistance when you tug on the kite's string to steer it. This resistance is the result of wind pressure. The wind pressure will pull the kite up and back, so hold the string tight!

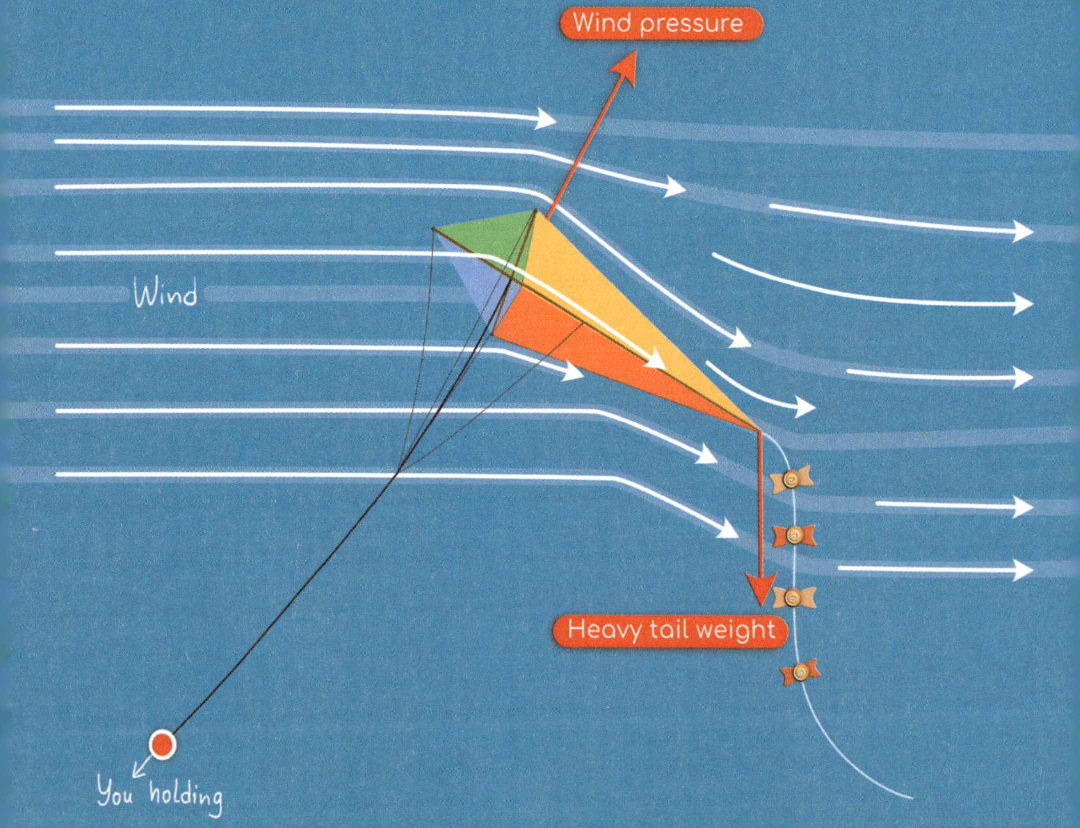

FRISBEE

WHAT'S THAT TOY?

The frisbee is a flying disc that was invented by Walter Frederick Morrison in 1955. Today, it's such a common toy that most of us would have played with one at some point or another. Here, we will focus on learning how the frisbee manages to stay in flight for so long.

LEVEL UP

GRASP THE PHYSICS CONCEPT

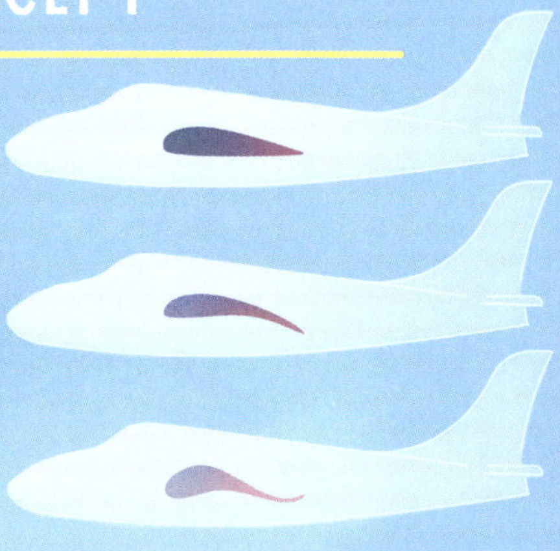

The first step to understanding the mystery of the frisbee's flight is to take a look at how the wings of an airplane work. What we learnt in the last chapter about how the wind holds a kite in the sky will help us to understand the physics behind flying.

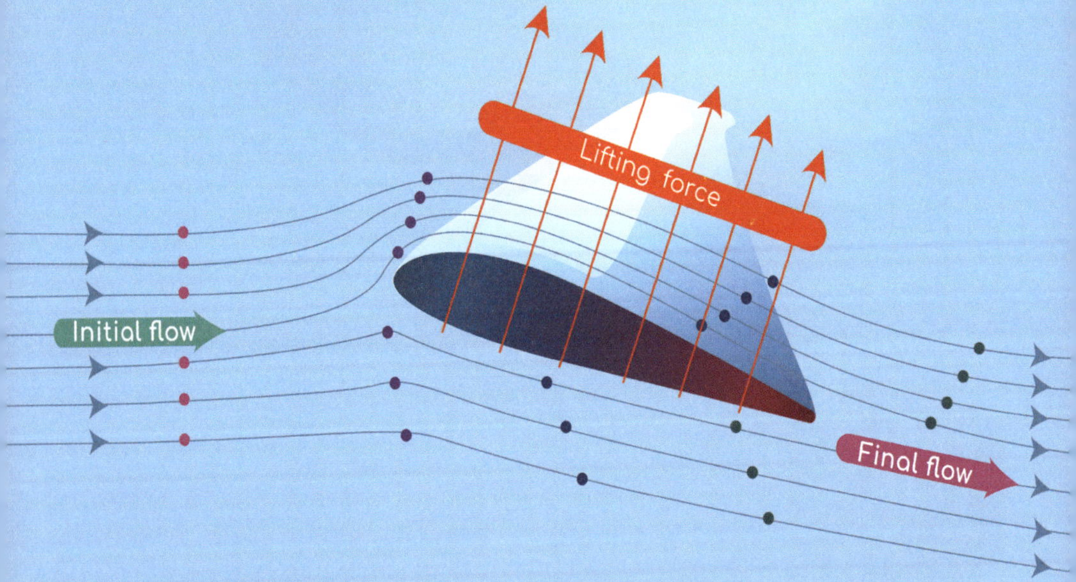

An airplane's wing redirects the airstream to produce a lift. It does this by deflecting air, which causes the direction of the airflow to tilt downwards.

Meanwhile, the airflow counteracts that tilting which produces lift. Even a small change in the direction of the airflow can cause a significant force to act on the wing's surface, because the plane is travelling at a high velocity. For example, commercial airplanes typically travel between 600 to 900 kilometres per hour, pushing down around 200 tons of air each second.

BONUS LEVEL

The sails of a ship work in a similar way, by deflecting the airstream to produce force. The difference in this case is that the sails do not lift the ship, of course, but pull it across the water.

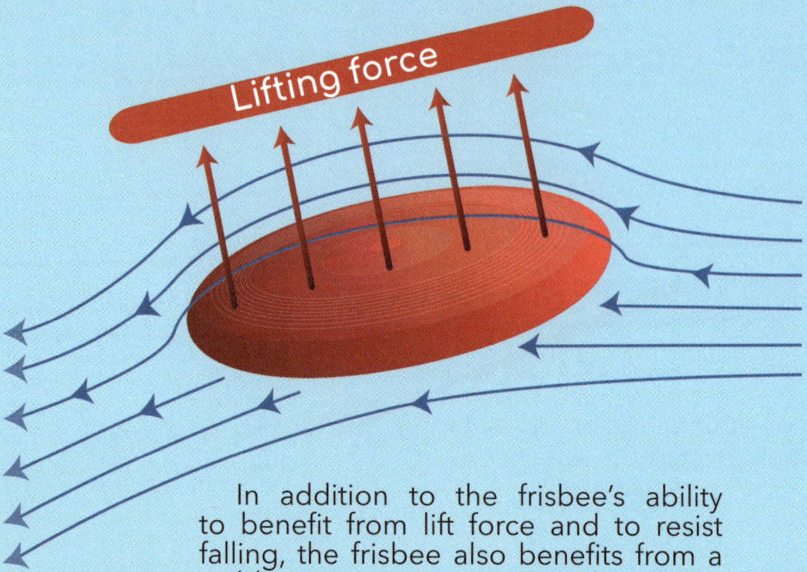

In addition to the frisbee's ability to benefit from lift force and to resist falling, the frisbee also benefits from a stable rotation pattern. Together, these factors make it possible to create long and elegant throws.

However, it's important to note that sometimes even the most beautifully-planned frisbee throws are spoiled by unexpected turbulence. Turbulence – the unsteady movements that occur naturally in air streams or liquid streams – can be hard to predict.

You may have experienced it for yourself, if you've ever flown in an airplane and been jolted by unexpected bumps! As a result of turbulence, a frisbee's flight path can be affected by a sudden dramatic change in lift force.

There is one more effect to consider: if you had superhuman eyesight and you were to look down on the frisbee from above, you would notice that the air surrounding the frisbee rotates along with the frisbee as it spins. This occurs because the air is in contact with the frisbee.

In fact, air – just like any other liquid or gas – slightly sticks to everything it touches.

Due to this effect, the airstream above the frisbee is accelerated by the plane rotation, and the airstream beneath it is slowed. Like the sails of a ship, the deflected airstream creates a pulling force (known as the Magnus force), which causes the frisbee to turn as it flies. This effect is usually small.

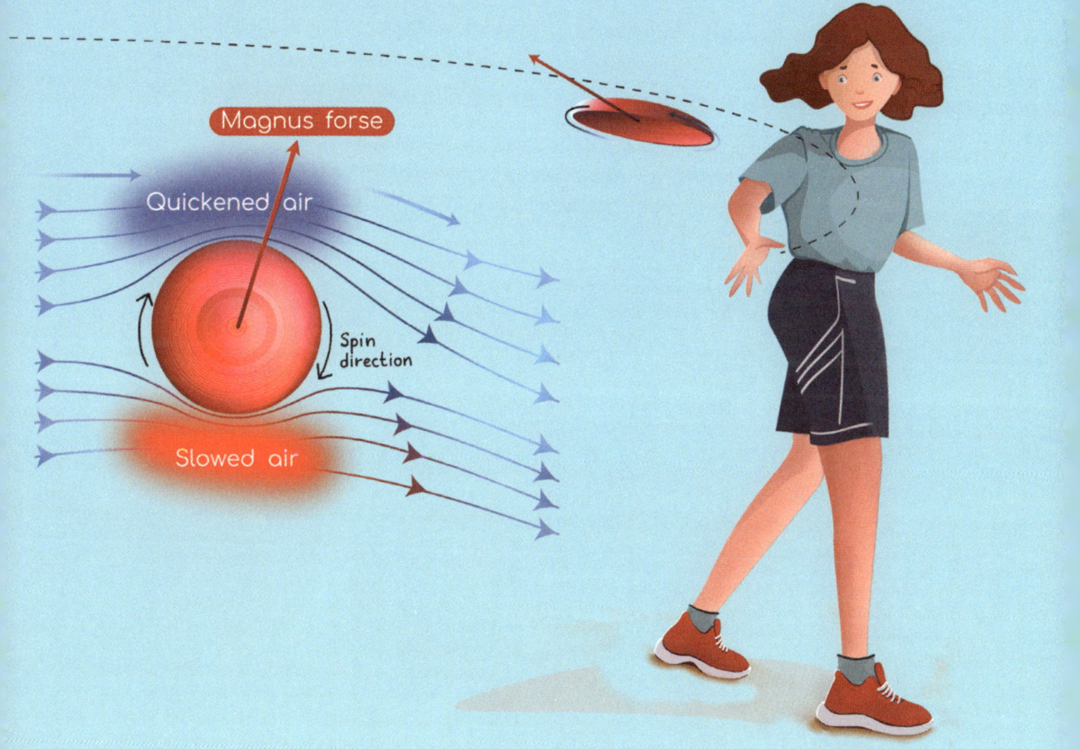

BONUS LEVEL CAN YOU DO THIS?

Now, armed with the knowledge above, why not go outside and try a game of Ultimate Frisbee? It's a sport that feels like a hybrid of football and soccer, with two teams and two goal zones. Points are scored by throwing the frisbee to a teammate in the goal zone. The team with the most points wins. Experiment with different throws, and use your understanding of the physics behind the frisbee to give you an edge in the game!

The Magnus force is used to the frisbee player's advantage when performing throws, such as the "scoober", the "hammer" and the "thumber".

WALK-ALONG GLIDER

WHAT'S THAT TOY?

The walk-along glider is a very light flatish glider, first proposed in 1955 by Joseph E. Grant. Since the original walk-along glider was invented, there have been many different variations. In this chapter, we'll learn about the most common one, which you can build at home yourself!

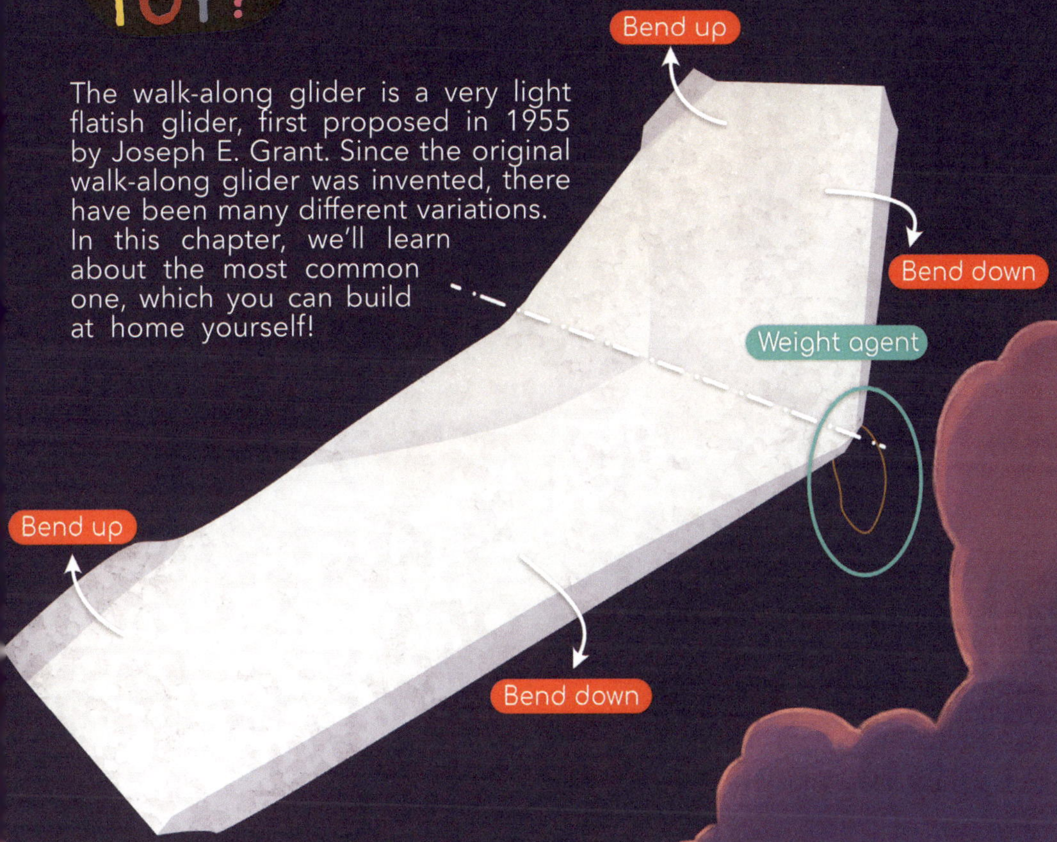

The most important part of building a walk-along glider is to find the right materials. The glider has to be very light, but strong. Paper-thin slices of styrofoam will do the trick!

LEVEL UP PHYSICS AT PLAY

When you release the walk-along glider, it floats through the air for quite a long time before it eventually falls to the ground.

How does it manage to stay in the air for so long? The walk-along glider operates as a plane wing or kite.

However, sometimes it is assumed that it flies due to air resistance, like a parachute.

A parachute slows the descent of falling objects by making use of air resistance. Air resistance works like this: imagine a parachute falling to the earth. The air particles beneath the parachute cannot simply pass through it, so they end up bouncing off it.

Countless particles reflect off the parachute, then collide with other neighbouring particles in a ping-pong effect. This creates a great deal of pressure (or air resistance), which acts opposite to gravity, slowing the descent.

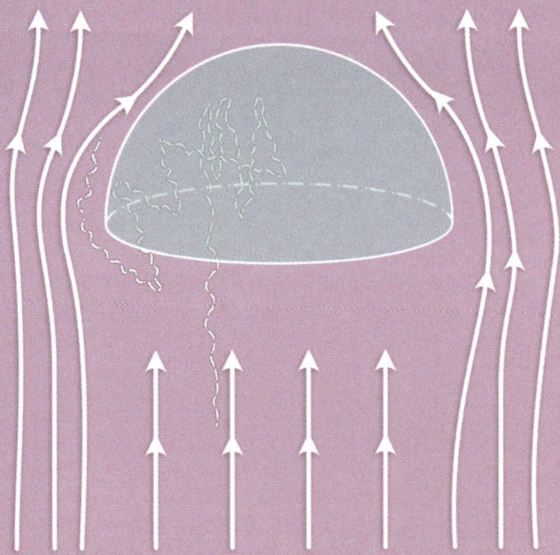

A kite, however, works by making use of the lifting force that appears when airflow changes direction (if you need a refresher, have a look at the chapter titled "Kite").

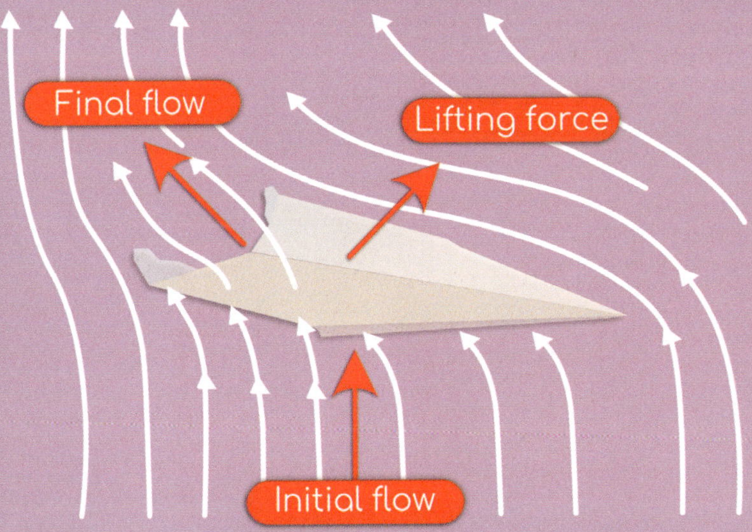

BONUS LEVEL CAN YOU DO THIS?

What do you think we could do to hold the glider in the air for a while? Well, we could blow on it from below – that would certainly create an upwards airstream and a lift force that would allow our glider to stay in the air!

But there's a much better way: to redirect the airflow, simply walk along behind the glider holding a flat board that is tilted away from your body.

This will push the air upwards, towards the underbelly of the glider, creating an airflow that will keep the glider aloft. If you follow behind the glider, holding your board close to it and in the right position, the walk-along glider could fly forever… that is, until it flies into another object, such as a wall!

Practise flying your walk-along glider until you've gotten the hang of it, then experiment with the design. Try connecting two gliders, one on top of the other, using toothpicks. The glider should look a bit like a Colt plane. Does this new glider fly better than the simple version? Is it easier to control?

FUN FACTS

EFFORTLESS FLYING

Interesting fact: did you know that birds also use rising airstreams to soar effortlessly upward into the sky? When the wind blows towards mountains, for example, sometimes upward airflows are created.

Birds can then fly into the airstream and be carried high into the sky, almost without flapping.

BULLROARER

WHAT'S THAT TOY?

Have you ever heard of the bullroarer? Many people have never seen this simple toy which, at first glance, looks like nothing more than a ruler on a string. But as you'll soon see, the bullroarer is a lot of fun to play with!

To make your own, find a wooden ruler and carve two notches into either side of it. Next, you'll need to tie the string to the ruler using a fancy knot. Take a look at the illustration, and try to recreate the knot as carefully as you can. It's important to be very careful to tie the knot exactly as pictured, at the centre of the ruler, otherwise the toy won't work.

Now, it's time to make it fly!

BONUS LEVEL
CAN YOU DO THIS?

Hold the bullroarer by its string, allowing the ruler to hang down freely. Next, twist the ruler so that it begins to spin around the string. As it's spinning, swing the ruler in circular motions above your head, like a helicopter. You'll notice that the bullroarer begins to move above you in a cone-like shape, and it should buzz loudly. But why does the ruler spin?

PHYSICS AT PLAY

As air moves quickly over an object, it can turn, push or spin the object. Very much like with the wing of an airplane, a force is produced when the air deflects because of the object.

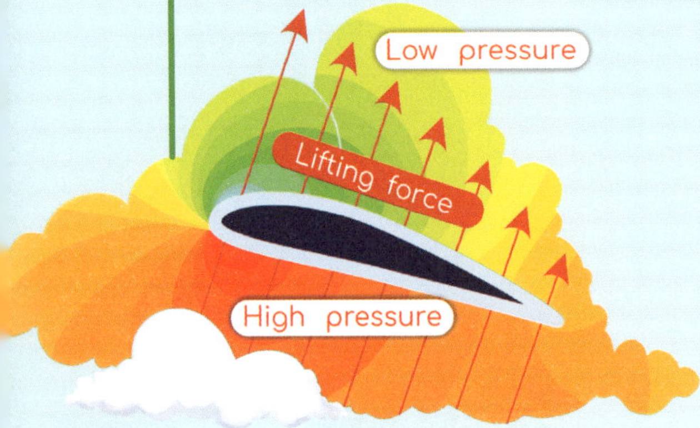

When this force is unevenly produced along the wing (or anything else), the difference in force produces torque. This torque tries to rotate the object, sometimes spinning it very fast, just like the bullroarer!

LEVEL UP

GRASP THE PHYSICS CONCEPT

Did you notice the strange buzzing noise coming from the bullroarer as it spins? Because the air is moving quickly and has little time to move around the object, vortices are produced behind the ruler.

When a liquid or gas (such as air) is spinning, we call it a vortex. Examples include tornadoes, or water flowing through a drain. The vortex can spin right or left (clockwise or counterclockwise).

In the illustration below, you can see the vortices appear, one by one. They spin in different directions, referred to as the vortex (a clockwise motion, seen here in red) and the anti-vortex (a counterclockwise motion, seen in blue). These vortices are what produce the buzzing sound!

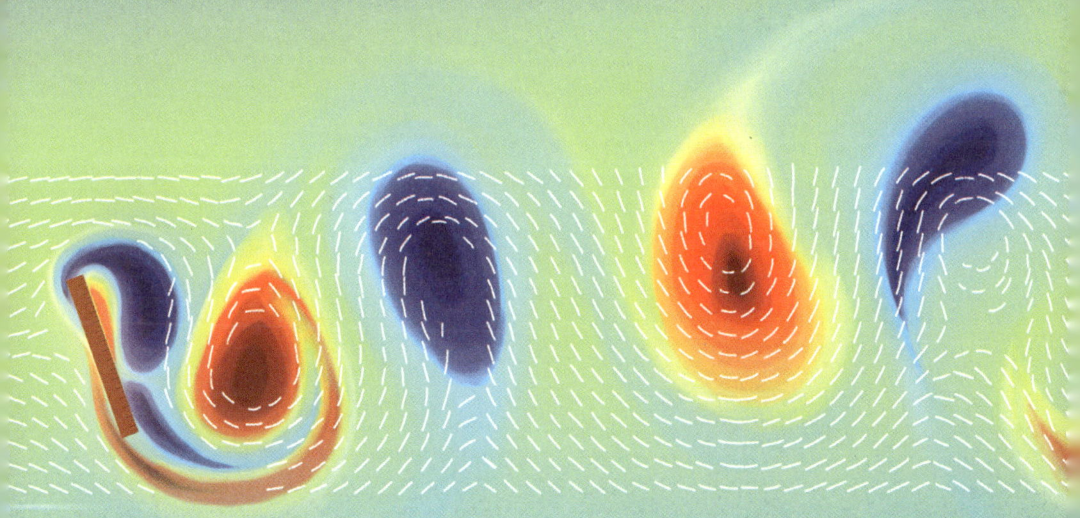

Did you happen to notice that the ruler moves in a cone-like manner when it is producing the sound? It does this because of the Magnus force. If the ruler spins clockwise, the cone will face downwards. If the ruler spins counterclockwise, the cone will face upwards.

You might have also seen that, from time to time, the sound will come and go. At the same time as the sound stops, the shape of the cone will change the direction it's facing. As we've just said, the shape of the cone depends on which direction you begin spinning the ruler. So, why does the cone flip?

The secret is in the string. The ruler is spinning very quickly, which ends up twisting the string. At some point, it becomes too difficult to continue twisting, so it stops, and the string begins unravelling in the opposite direction. That's why we see the cone flip.

TUMBLEWING

WHAT'S THAT TOY?

The tumblewing glider is dramatically different from most other aircraft, and it looks a bit like a spoiler on a sports car. John M. Collins first described this toy in 2004 in his book *Fantastic Flight*.

Let's start by making a tumblewing for ourselves to experiment with. To make your own tumblewing, all you'll need is a template, some newspaper and a pair of scissors.

BONUS LEVEL

CAN YOU DO THIS?

The template I've used here was inspired by one found on the "The Paper Airplane Guy" channel on YouTube.

First, carefully trace the tumblewing pattern onto a piece of newspaper, and then cut it out using a pair of scissors. After you've finished cutting out the pattern, all you need to do is to fold the sides. Now it's ready to use!

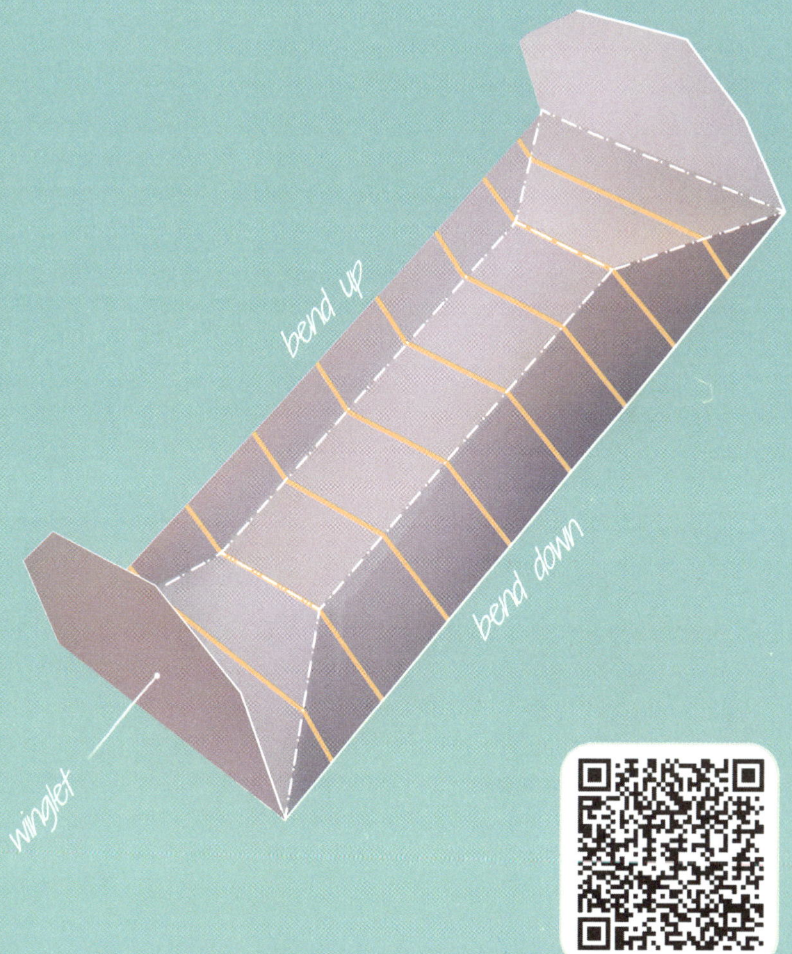

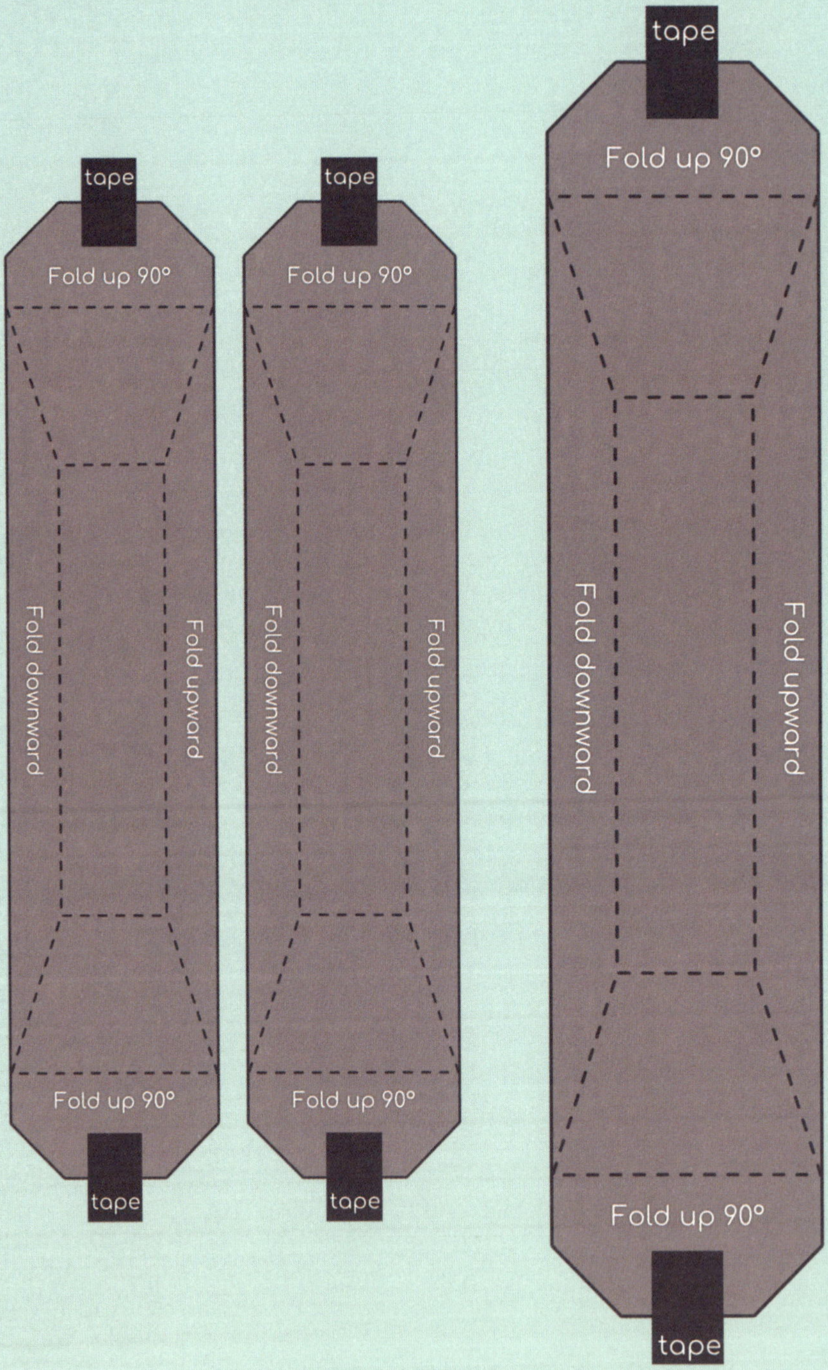
tape
Fold up 90°
Fold downward
Fold upward
Fold up 90°
tape
tape
Fold up 90°
Fold downward
Fold upward
Fold up 90°
tape
tape
Fold up 90°
Fold downward
Fold upward
Fold up 90°
tape

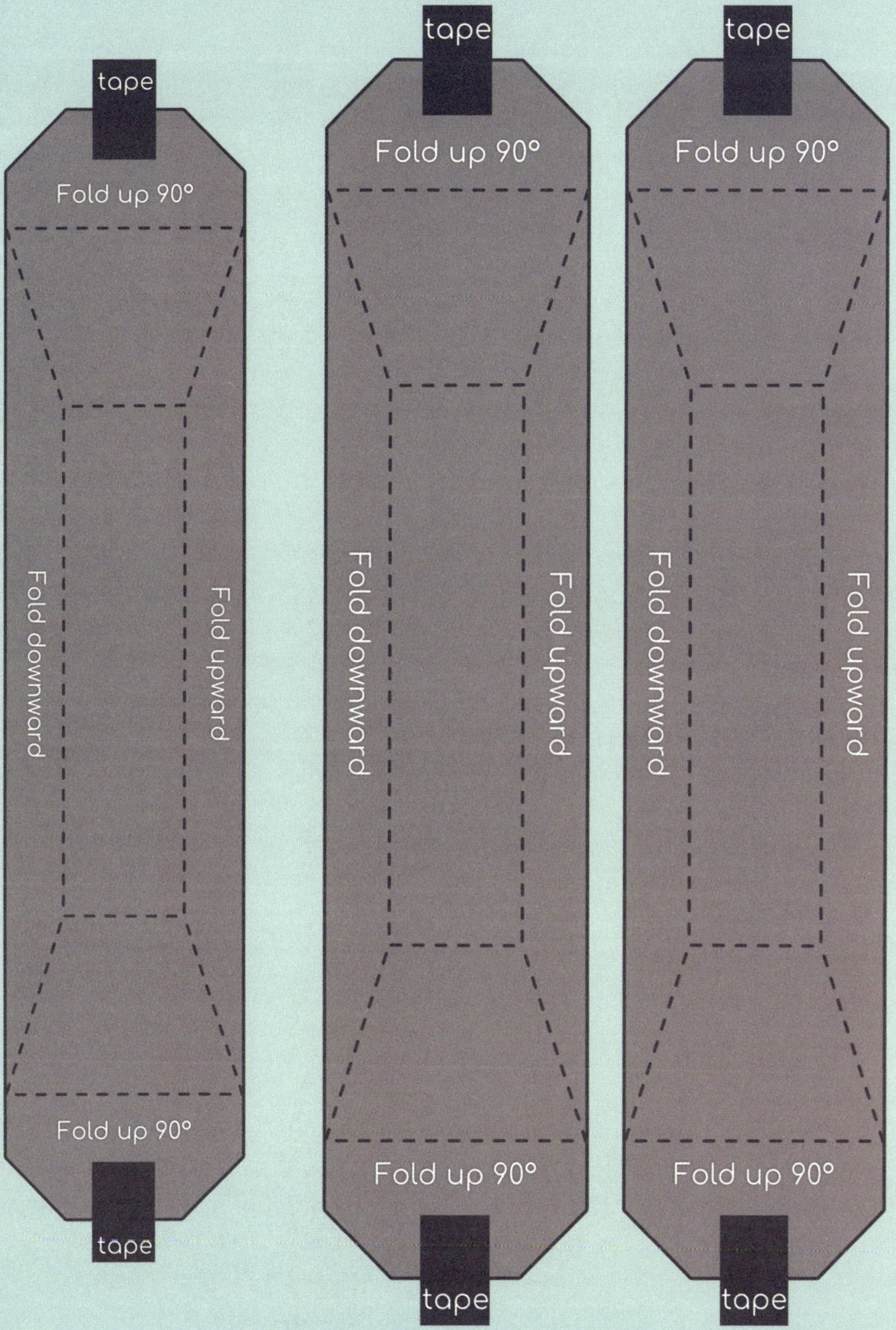
tape
Fold up 90°
Fold downward
Fold upward
Fold up 90°
tape
tape
Fold up 90°
Fold downward
Fold upward
Fold up 90°
tape
tape
Fold up 90°
Fold downward
Fold upward
Fold up 90°
tape

To launch the glider, simply hold it up and release it. After a short time, it will start to tumble and descend, spinning very quickly as it falls. Notice that it doesn't simply drop to the ground – it flies forward. The tumblewing is very impressive because it can stay in flight for a long time.

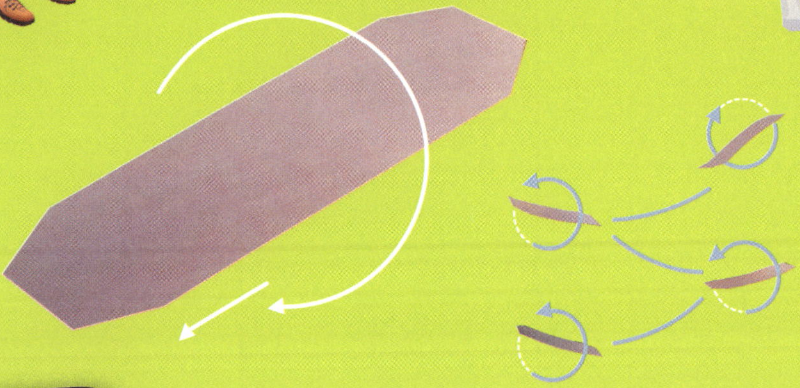

LEVEL UP

PHYSICS AT PLAY

Let's take a closer look at the tumblewing's design to see how it works. You might ask yourself, why are there so many folds? If you're curious to experiment, try cutting a simple strip of paper without folding it. Now hold it up high, and watch how it falls to the ground.

You'll see that the strip of paper spins a bit like the tumblewing, but over time it starts to lean to the right or the left before drifting to the ground, like a leaf.

Provide Stability

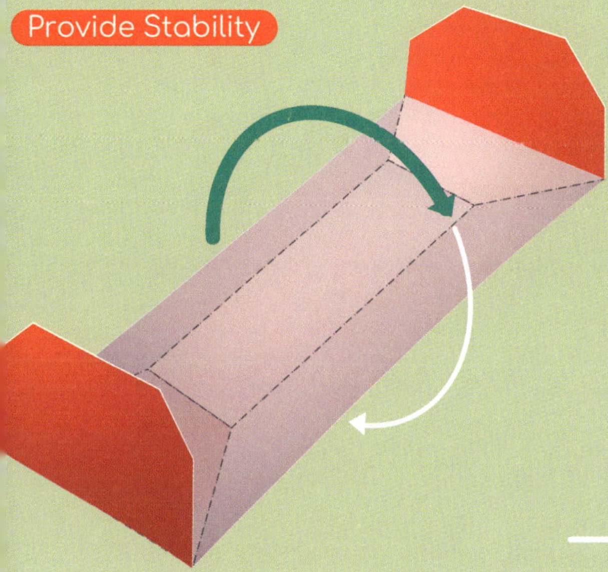

To prevent the paper from leaning to the left or right, we need to bend it on both sides. It doesn't really matter how you bend the paper – whether the bends face upwards or downwards, or whether they are on the same sides. The edges will add some stability to the paper as it falls.

Boost the rotation

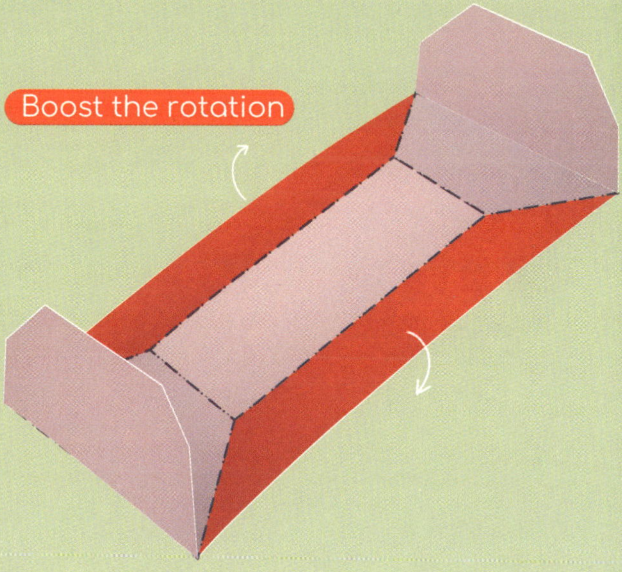

The folds along the long edges are not necessary, but adding them will help the tumblewing to rotate more easily and more quickly.

The next time you launch your tumblewing, try following behind it while holding the same flat board you used for the walk-along glider. If your tumblewing is small, this should work nicely to keep it in flight for a longer period of time. But if your tumblewing is too large, you may find this won't work quite as well.

Now, let's dive a bit deeper to see why the tumblewing falls to the ground so slowly. Most of the time, the tumblewing will fly like a parachute, or like a wing.

30°

LEVEL UP

PHYSICS AT PLAY

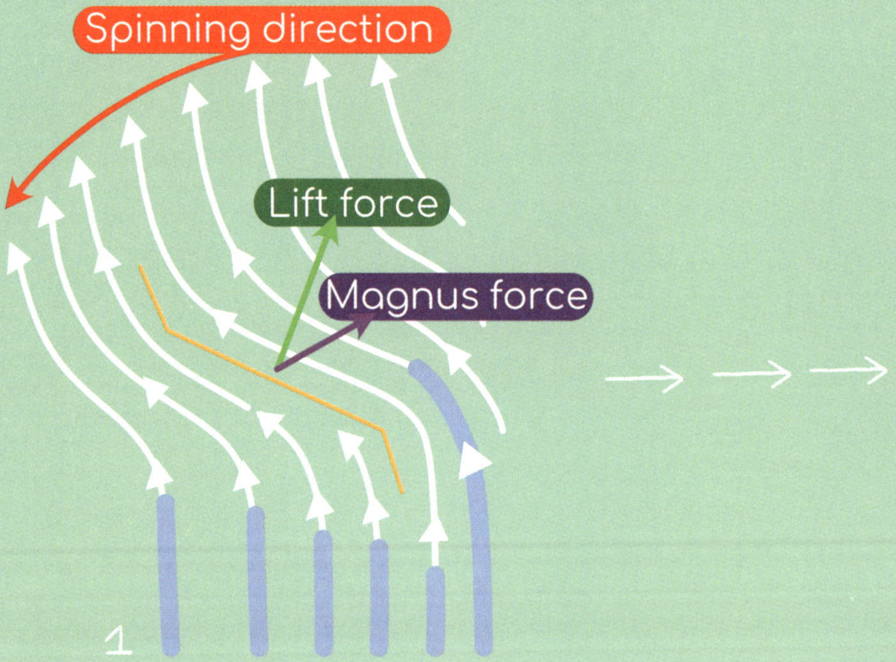

As the glider falls, a lift force (represented by the green arrow) acts on the tumblewing in a similar way as it would on a plane wing. This lift, unevenly produced along the glider, creates a torque, which causes the tumblewing to spin. As the wing is rotating, the Magnus force appears (represented by the purple arrow).

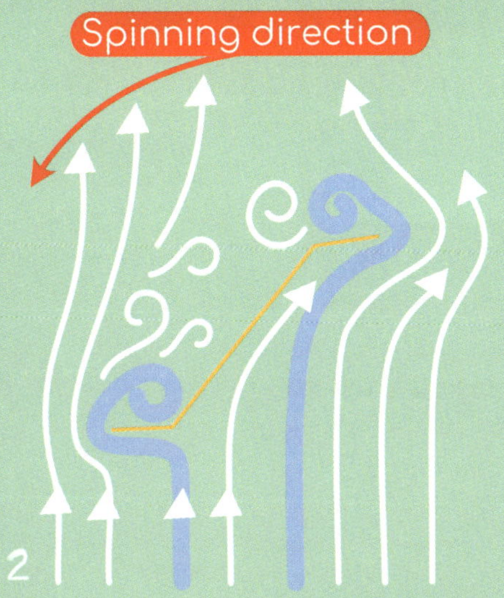

Together, the lift force and the Magnus force counteract gravity and delay the descent of the tumblewing. After some time, as the tumblewing falls, the "wing pattern" shifts to the "parachute pattern". Yet, the tumblewing continues spinning. Shortly afterward, the "parachute pattern" returns to the "wing pattern", and everything repeats. The tumblewing operates a bit like the bullroarer, although it rotates much slower.

Will a bigger glider fall faster or slower than a smaller one? Make three gliders of different sizes, and throw them one-by-one from the exact same height. Use a timer to record how long it takes for each to touch the ground. Did you guess correctly?

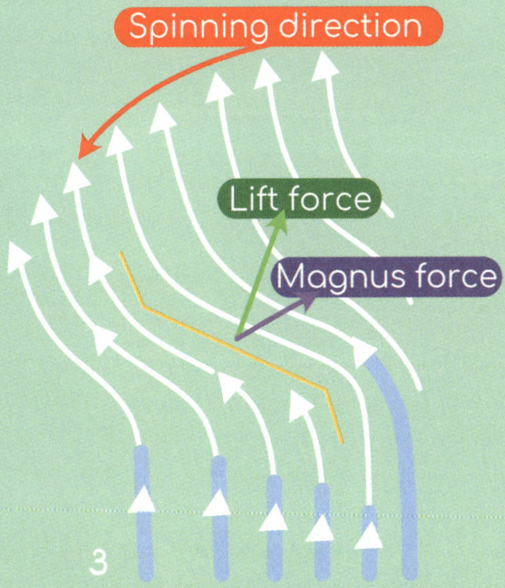

BOOMERANG

WHAT'S THAT TOY?

The boomerang is a powerful ancient weapon. Archaeologists have found many different varieties of boomerangs all over the world. The oldest known boomerang dates back to 10,000 BC and was found in South Australia.

Generally, there are two types of boomerangs: ones that return to their starting point, and ones that don't. The boomerangs that do not return are designed as weapons, and they fly far longer than the returning boomerangs.

The hunting boomerang, also known as a throwing stick or a "kylie", looks like a long stick. You can think of the kylie as the parent of a standard boomerang.

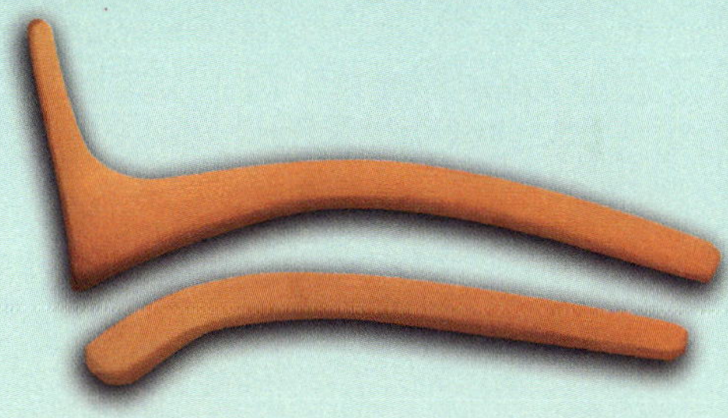

The specially calibrated surface gives it incredible aerodynamic stability. The kylie can fly on a long, straight path for up to 70 metres! And even at its maximum distance, it's still moving fast enough to easily hunt prey.

Similar tools can be found in various parts of the world. For example, the ancient Egyptians used throwing sticks for hunting small game such as rabbits, ducks and other birds. The indigenous people of Australia used it to hunt kangaroos, wallabies and emus from a great distance.

Now, having explored a bit of the history behind the boomerang, let's take a look at the physics behind the classic returning boomerang.

LEVEL UP

PHYSICS AT PLAY

You might think of the boomerang as a flying object with two wings. And as we've already learnt, when a wing is positioned in a stream of moving air, lift force appears. The boomerang's two wings face in different directions – one looks forward, and the other backward.

After the boomerang is thrown, it begins to spin. The effect of spinning is that the relative air stream moves faster on one side than the other, resulting in a lift force that is different on both sides.

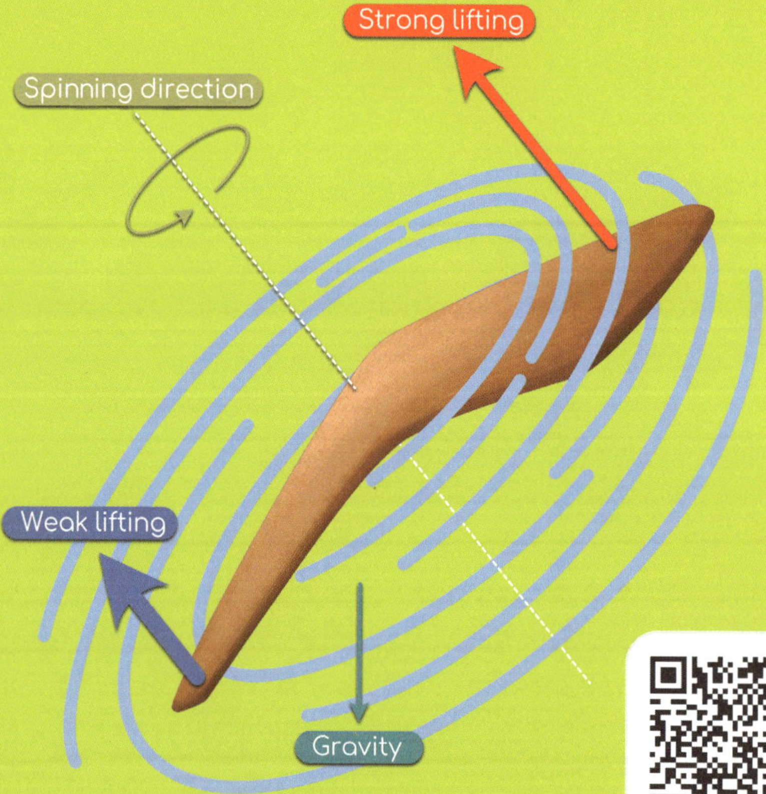

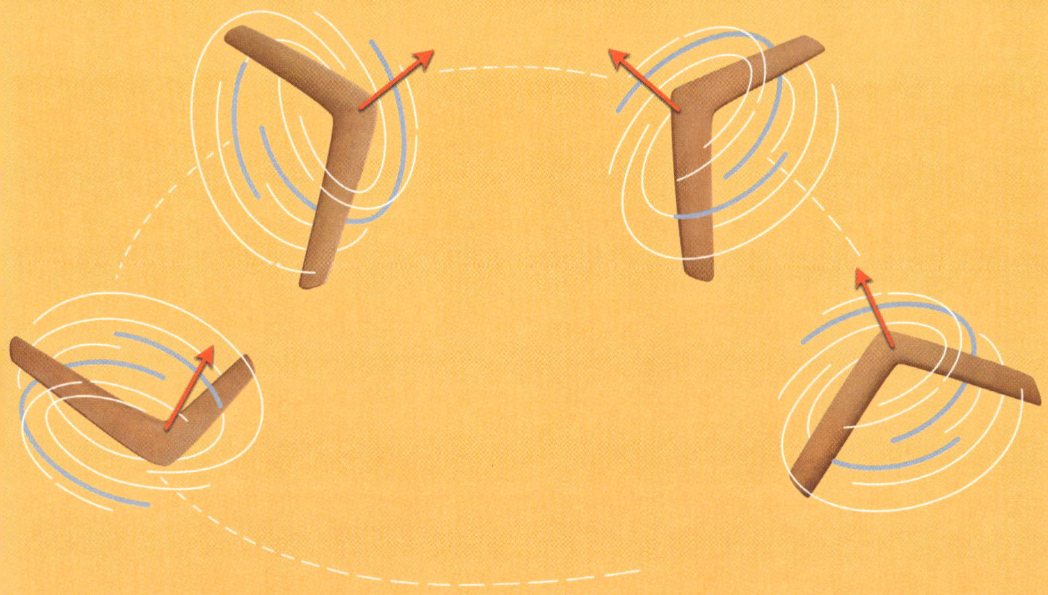

This is actually a very important point, because the difference in force creates torque. This torque changes the angular momentum of the boomerang, which causes it to come back.

As a result of this torque, the boomerang has a gyroscopic precession. This rotation (or "precession"), along with horizontal lift force, causes the boomerang to return to the place it was thrown from.

There are many factors that can be adjusted to change the boomerang's flight path. For example, if you change the size of the boomerang's wings, or the angle between them, this can dramatically change the boomerang's flight pattern. There is even a sort of boomerang that can fly in a figure eight pattern!

MIRASCOPE

WHAT'S THAT TOY?

In 1969, Pierre Caliste Landry, a janitor at the University of California, Santa Barbara, was cleaning the physics department. The department served as storage space for a variety of equipment, including a large surplus of searchlight mirrors from World War II.

These concave mirrors would have been placed behind a light bulb to produce a beam of light. They were stacked on top of each other for storage, probably because this was the most compact and efficient means of storing them without scratching the mirrors.

When Landry began to dust the top of the stacked searchlights, he was confused because he could not seem to get rid of the dust. He soon realised that there actually was no dust – it had merely been an optical illusion!

Sometime later, Landry discussed his observations with Professor Virgil Elings. Together, just one year later, they patented the "Optical Display Device", or Mirascope.

The Mirascope was constructed of two parabolic mirrors, one placed on top of the other. "Parabolic" means that the form of the object is curved inward, a bit like a spoon. The top mirror has a hole where the illusion will appear, and the centre of the lower mirror serves as a platform for an object. As soon as an object is placed on the lower mirror, the optical illusion emerges!

LEVEL UP PHYSICS AT PLAY

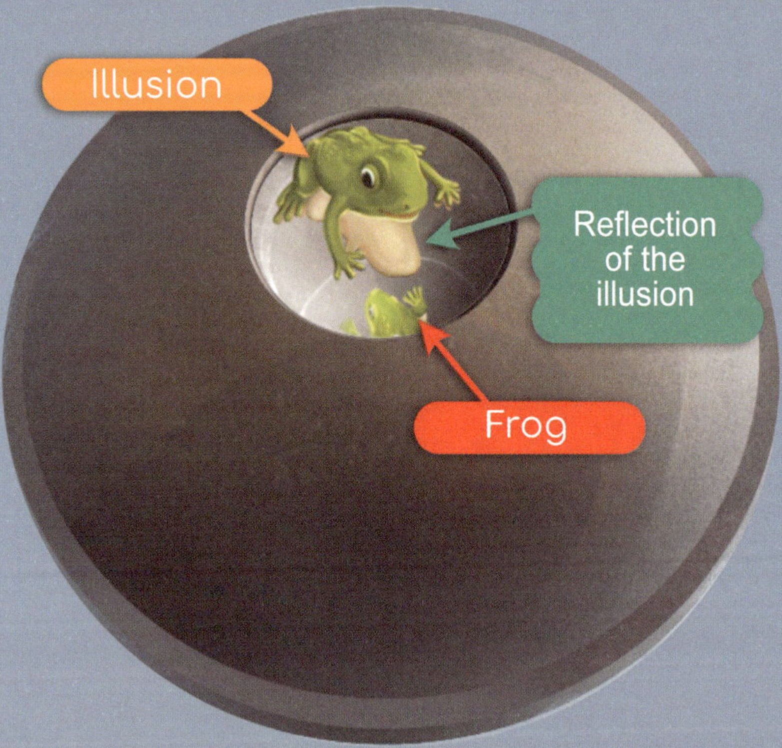

If you place a toy frog at the bottom of the mirascope, you will see three frogs. Only one of them is real. There are two illusions: one at the top, and another underneath, which appears to be a reflection of the first.

The optical reflection within the Mirascope causes you to see a frog where there isn't one. The same effect could be achieved with a simple mirror. If you've ever been inside a hall of mirrors at an amusement park or funfair, you will have experienced this optical illusion for yourself. It can be easy to mistake a reflection for a real person!

In a curved mirror, such as the Mirascope, the law of reflection is exactly the same as for a flat mirror: the angle of incidence equals the angle of reflection. However, now our calculations have to take into account the tangent (perpendicular) plane of the mirror at the point of contact.

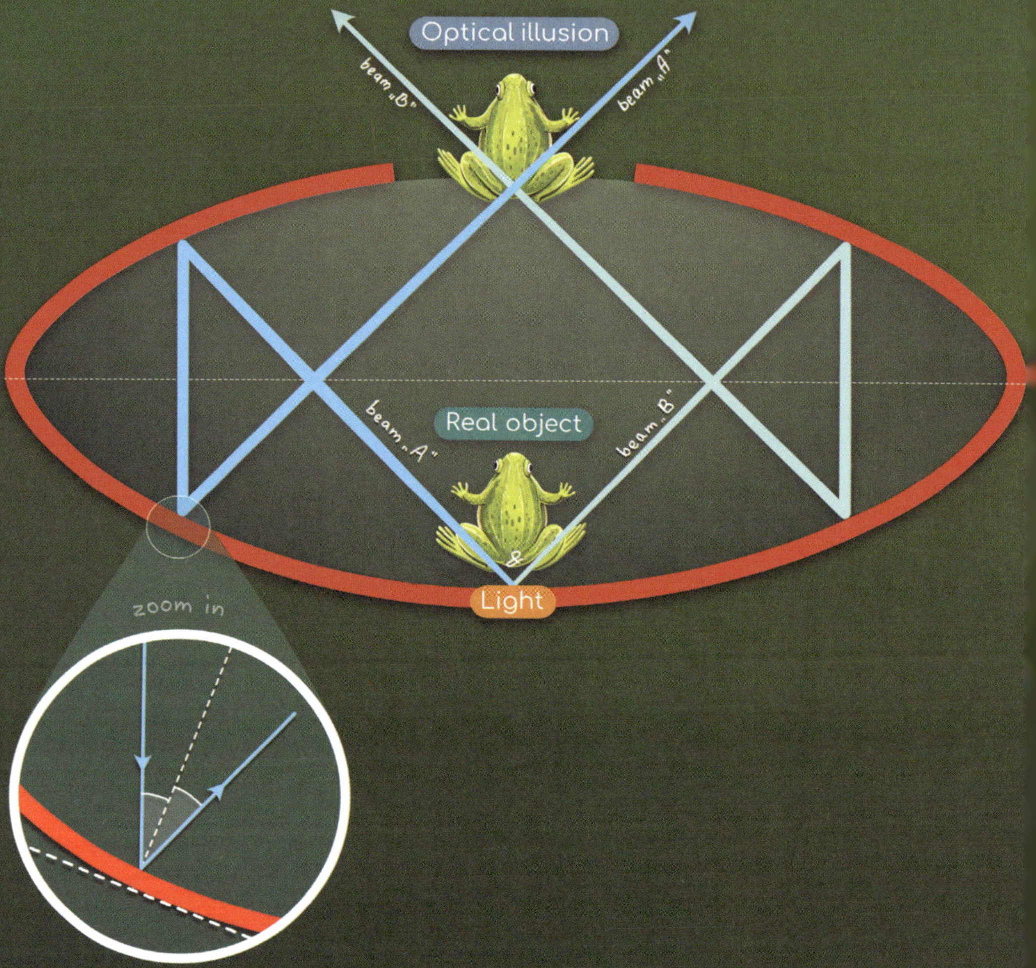
Optical illusion
beam "B"
beam "A"
Real object
beam "A"
beam "B"
Light
zoom in

Let's take a closer look at how the Mirascope works: first, take any two points of the frog, such as the frog's leg and head. Imagine that both the head and leg radiate beams of light. Now try to predict how those beams of light would leave the mirascope.

If the beams from the frog's head cross at the top of the Mirascope and maintain the same relative angles as they had in the beginning, our eyes would see the head as being located at the top of the Mirascope. The same logic should be applied to the leg. If the reflected image of the frog has the same size and shape, our brains perceive the reflected image as the actual frog. When this is achieved regardless of your viewing angle, our brains are tricked into thinking that a reflected image is, in fact, a 3D object!

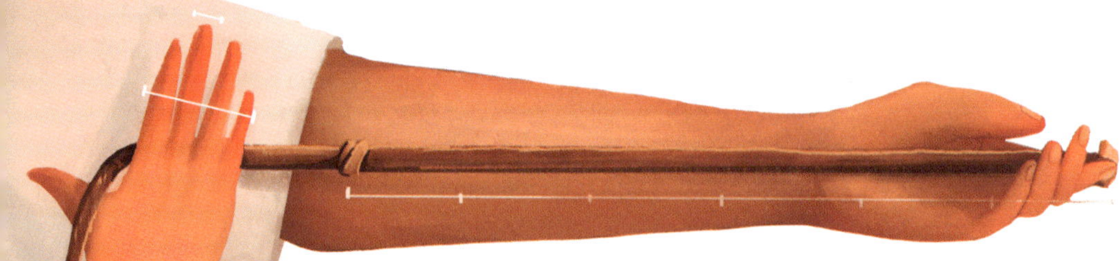

AFTERWORD

This book was the result of three fortunate events. The first occurred during my undergraduate years, when I worked as a physics tutor for children in the 5th and 6th grades. I was trained by the brilliant and creative minds of Oleksandr Trilis (a physicist) and Dmytro Basov (a mathematician). Many would argue that it is almost impossible to teach physics to such young children, but Trilis and Basov proved otherwise!

Though Trilis and Basov mastered the technique of teaching younger students, new teachers often struggle to teach physics to young pupils. This book was, in part, created to meet the need for lessons tailored to young minds.

A couple of years later, after the Max Planck Institute invited me to continue my scientific study as a PhD student, I decided that, before I left Ukraine, I would write this book to pay forward the opportunities and knowledge I had been fortunate enough to receive. I started to write, but the product was a hardly-readable disaster. I decided to put the project aside for awhile.

After arriving in Germany to start my PhD research, my supervisor, Inti Sodemann, suggested that I begin writing a scientific paper to practise my writing, as writing is very important in science. I followed that advice, but once again, I discovered I needed to work on my writing skills. At that point, I remembered my postponed book project and thought this would be the perfect way to improve my writing and narrative skills!

I realised that I could not finish something I wasn't interested in, and instructions weren't my thing. Instead I found myself walking around with toys in my pocket, playing with them and showing them to people. On my first Christmas in Germany, aged 23, I learned about the advent calendar – the second fortunate event! Having a couple of toys in my pockets, I realised that I could make an advent calendar of my own, with small toys, simple instructions and lessons about physics – a little like Kinder Surprise toys. This was the beginning of the book you see today.

I told Inti about the idea for this book, and his excitement spurred me on – the third event. When Roderich Moessner, the Director of the Max Planck Institute for the Physics of Complex Systems, immediately offered his support, it was clear that this book was worth writing, and I would finish it. I am very grateful to everyone involved in the process, and I sincerely hope you enjoy reading it.

ACKNOWLEDGMENTS

I want to thank my closest relatives: my mother and brother, who have provided endless support to me in pursuing my interests. And, of course, to my wife, Anastasiia, who is my greatest support and inspiration. Her overwhelming excitement makes my work feel much more meaningful.

Here, I want to thank many friends, teachers and previous bosses who have contributed to this book.

I want to thank the outstanding scientist, Inti Sodemann, who continuously inspired me to push forward and finish this project. I owe an enormous debt of gratitude to Inti, who taught and counselled me. He gave freely of his time to discuss physics and life. He pushed me to develop my projects and ideas, and without his support I would not have been able to finish this book.

I want to thank my dear friend, Nikolay Semeniakin, who contributed a lot to the project by providing me with advice on all aspects of the book. It is a great pleasure to have such a competent and close friend who is always ready to help.

I express my gratitude to Paul McClarty, who generously provided his time and energy to contribute to this project. I deeply admire his curiosity and comprehensive knowledge as a scientist, and the valuable suggestions he made as I was writing this book.

I also want to thank Oleksandr Trilis and Dmytro Basov, along with the 5 Sciences educational project, for providing the initial inspiration for this book.

I want to acknowledge my friends and mentors who have made various contributions to this book or supported me during the project: Oleksandr Trilis, Dmytro Basov, Oleksandr Yakimenko, Oleg Barabash, Inti Sodemann, Falko Pientka, Jun Yung Khoo, Peng Rao, Olga Maliyta, Alexander Nachlenko, Maxim Litovchenko, Yevgenia Cheipesh, Janette Jakob and Daria Tsapok. I would like to especially thank Miroslava Slusar, who has been so cheerful and energetic, always willing to help with the design and illustrations in this book.

Finally, as this book project was being concluded, disaster befell my homeland, Ukraine. I am at a loss for words to describe the admiration and gratitude I feel for those brave people in Ukraine who put their lives on the line to defend everybody's right to live in freedom and peace.

WHAT IS NEXT?

If you enjoyed this book, the following resources may be of interest as you delve deeper into the world of physics.

The works of Yakov Perelman, including:

- *Mathematics Can Be Fun*
- *Recreational Astronomy*
- *Physics for Entertainment*
- *Figures for Fun*
- *Fun with Maths & Physics*
- *Arithmetic for Entertainment*
- *Mechanics for Entertainment*
- *Geometry for Entertainment*
- *Astronomy for Entertainment*
- *Lively Mathematics*
- *Physics Everywhere*
- *Tricks and Amusements*
- *Algebra Can be Fun*

The works of Stephen Hawking:

- *A Brief History of Time*
- *Brief Answers to the Big Questions*
- *My Brief History*
- *The Grand Design*
- *Black Holes and Baby Universe and Other Essays*
- *The Universe in a Nutshell*
- *God Created the Integers*
- *On the Shoulders of Giants*

And from Neil deGrasse Tyson:

- *Astrophysics for People in a Hurry*
- *Death by Black Hole*
- *Letters from an Astrophysicist*
- *Welcome to the Universe*
- *Astrophysics for Young People in a Hurry*

FURTHER READING

For more home experiments, don't miss the following website: https://sciencetoymaker.org.

And finally, if you would like to consult some original research articles and journals, I recommend:

1. *Physics Education*, an international journal targeted at those who teach physics to students aged 11 and up.

   As well as the following two scientific articles targeting the physics behind Euler's disk:

2. Moffatt, H.K., 2000. "Euler's disk and its finite-time singularity." Nature, 404(6780), pp.833-834.

3. Villanueva, R. and Epstein, M., 2005. "Vibrations of Euler's disk." Physical Review E, 71(6), p.066609.

These are just a few examples of published papers relevant to the content in this book. It is my hope that they may inspire some readers to begin a career in science. Who knows – maybe one day you will publish your own scientific paper!